Cindy & John

America Asks Bruce

■ Radio's #1 answer man,
Bruce Williams, gives practical
answers to everyday problems

Mainstreet Productions, Inc.
San Diego, California

Mainstreet Productions, Inc.
8745 Aero Drive - Suite 105
San Diego, CA 92123

To readers who are fellow listeners:

Like you, we've listened to Bruce over the years and are not only wiser for it, we're Bruce Williams "street wise." We would never buy or sell a house without an attorney (even though we reside in California) and we would never buy a used car without having a mechanic inspect it first. And beyond the useful advice, while being fascinated and entertained, our spirits are buoyed just knowing that there are people out there with problems just as troublesome as ours.

There were just too many times, however, when there wasn't quite enough dust on the dashboard to write down exactly what Bruce said about something important, so we could quote him when we got home.

There were just too many times when we wished our friends heard what Bruce had to say about....opening a lamp shop... or fighting it out with a condo association. There were just too many times when we wished we could look up Bruce's answers in a *book*.

With that idea in mind, armed with some of Bruce's famous advice, we published this one.

We hope you enjoy reading it and re-reading it.

Dennis Regan   Geoffrey T. Williams

MAINSTREET PRODUCTIONS, INC.

For the past six-plus years it has been my privilege to talk to my friends and neighbors around the country one-on-one. Unlike many fine talk presenters, I have yet to have my first guest. No makers and shakers, none of the great authors, just friends discussing their mutual concerns and problems. Let's face it, that's what life is all about. Solutions allow us to enjoy a little better life with less hassle.

Many of us agonize over decisions for hours, days, even weeks, and come to find out that the problem that seemed so important at the time really had little impact on our lives. On other occasions we make a snap decision that has profound influence. The troublesome part of this equation is that it is difficult at the time to determine which situation is trivial and which is profound. I have tried to adopt the approach with my listeners that if it is important to them, it is important to me. That is not to say that if I feel that they are getting all uptight over something that is really of small consequence, that I'm not going to point this out. I think that's part of my job. It is not part of my job to make friends. I like to believe that I have been successful in doing so, but if the choice has to be made between being friendly and chastising the caller so that there is absolutely no question about where I stand, I choose the latter course every time.

The printed word is a bit different. You have the opportunity to read, reread, and read again if you choose, until you are absolutely certain of the meaning. This is not true on the air. It's my contention that it must be clear to the listener precisely where I stand. Not only to the person with whom I'm having the conversation, but, more importantly, to a significantly larger number who may be eavesdropping on the conversation.

It would be ingenuous of me to say I wasn't complemented when Mainstreet Productions approached me with the thought of distilling hundreds of hours of my program into book form. Complemented, yes, but not at all sure that the result would be worth while. I was agreeably surprised when the publishers took a sample of our programming and provided me with a taste of what was to become the menu. In particular I was pleased with the idea of cross referencing. It should be abundantly clear that nothing I say is written in stone. It is my thought that if I can stimulate you, the listener and reader, into thinking out your situation thoroughly before you act and, hopefully, entertain you in the process, I have accomplished my mission.

So called "common sense" can be a very uncommon commodity. I try to empathize with my correspondents. I do my best to put myself in their position and then respond as I would respond given that stimulation. The course of action I may be inclined to take is not necessarily the one for you. I can only point out to you that this is one possible solution to your situation. If I've encouraged you to think of things in a less direct fashion, recognizing that there are "many ways to skin a cat," then I think you will find this book helpful. Summarized, if I have one goal I hope I can "drive you to think".

Bruce Williams
1988

CONTENTS

CHAPTER 1 *Taxes*

" You waved a big red flag right in their face. If I were working for the IRS, I would have seen that flag wave and I would have come after you. "

Because we're minors operating a small business, do we have to register with anybody?

I'm 14 years old and I have a partner who's an ace at programming. He's 13. We have started a small business - programming computers and setting up software. Do we have to worry about taxes? Since we both operate out of our homes with our own equipment can the overhead be deducted? And will our parents' home owner's policy cover the equipment, even if we do use it for a business?

■If you are providing a service I do not know that you have to register with anybody. I don't think being a minor is an issue.

You still have to pay taxes. Presently, if you make more then $3,000 you have to file. You may need to file a quarterly return with the IRS in addition to a regular annual income tax form just like everybody else. You'll have to pay Social Security tax, income tax, the whole nine yards. Your parents should be able to help you there. Overhead can be deducted. I believe you'll have no problem with insurance coverage, but there may be a dollar limit. Check with your parents' agent. Also, since you probably will operate out of your homes, ask a tax person about deducting some of your overhead.

How can I convince the IRS they're wrong and allow me a deduction that I can prove I'm entitled to?

I prepared my own taxes. The IRS is questioning a loss I declared in an oil lease program in which I invested during the latter part of December. They are coming back and saying that I cannot claim it in 1983 because I wrote the check in 1982. I sent them the information from the leasing company showing that it's a special 1983 program.

■If you were looking to get a lot of information about machine tools, would you hire a plumber? What I'm saying to you is that this is a technical area requiring a technician. That means somebody who stays abreast of tax laws, understands them and practices before the IRS. That is not you.

Trying to defend your position by showing them what the company says about an investment program will not get you anywhere. What the vendor of the tax shelter says means nothing. It is what the IRS says that counts.

They are questioning a tax shelter. You waved a big red flag right in their face. If I were working for the IRS, I would have seen that flag wave and I would have come after you.

How can I protect my mother from any liability for a business she's investing in?

I am purchasing a business and I'm borrowing half of the money from my mom. I want to insure that she gets her money back in the event the business fails. My idea is to make her a 51% partner.

■If you're really serious about limiting your mother's liability in regards to your business, the last thing you want to do is put her name on it. I'll tell you why.

What if things go sour and you can't make the payments. You can't pay your taxes. Who do they go after? Dear ol' mom. So, you are not doing her any favors by making her a 51% partner.

What you should do is give your mother a second mortgage on the property. And do not move an inch putting this deal together without an attorney on your side. The people you're buying the business from will have one.

Should I give our kids a gift of $10,000 to put down on a house or just buy a house and rent it to them?

We do not know what the tax ramifications are. An accountant told us that it's really a no-no to buy a house and rent it to your kids. We just want to help them, but we do not want to get ourselves into a bind.

■It would be more tax help for them if you gave them the money. There is no tax benefit if they rent. Any tax benefit will accrue only to you. They could write off the interest on payments, but they could not write off what they paid for rent. On the other hand, if you buy, you'll be able to depreciate the house and achieve some tax benefits.

I don't agree with your accountant about renting to your children. You do have to charge a fair market rent. It is true that if you rent it to them for a $1.00 a year and then try to depreciate the building, that is a no-no. But, if the house is worth $50,000 and you charge them $500 per month, which is about right on a $50,000 house, there would be no problem. Again, however, I'm not recommending that route.

There is another alternative. You could loan the money to them, interest free, if it's under $10,000. If your husband is alive, you can give them up to $40,000 per year. If it were me, I would loan them the money for a second mortgage.

Will the IRS make a friend pay income taxes on the interest I pay him for a loan?

A friend gave me a $10,000 interest free loan for a year and said pay it back when you can.

■Anybody can give to anybody $10,000 a year and there is no taxable event. Anything over $10,000 is taxable to the donor. So, as I understand it, as long as he gives you the interest too, you are home free. You can give it back to him whenever you want to.

How do I handle sales tax for my photography business?

I started photographing weddings and charging a small fee. I don't charge state or federal tax. I add that amount on to my taxes at the end of the year.

■If your state has sales tax, you're obliged to collect it. And you can get into some serious hot water if you don't. I must believe that wedding pictures are subject to sales tax.

Welcome to the real world. You have to get yourself a Federal ID number. You have to get a state sales tax number and do all of the things that real business people do. You don't have to pay for the number. They give it to you free...so they can keep track of you. How you pay varies in each state depending on the amount of money you collect. If you collect a very small amount of money, I think you just pay quarterly. But the vast majority of small businesses pay monthly. If you happen to get into something that really brings in the bread, then you have to pay weekly.

Will I have to wait six months from December to avoid capital gains tax from the sale of stock?

And will I have to pay income tax on the total amount or just the dividends? The value of my shares went from $4,000 to $9,000. I bought some stock with a friend under his name and his account number. In the summer he turned my shares over to me in my name through the company and I received my shares of the stock.

■Your acquisition was the date the stock was put in your name. So if you are talking about capital gains, sure, I can't imagine any other way.

If you realize a gain from the sale of this stock, you are going to have to pay ordinary income on the whole thing.

Would it be advantageous to change my corporation to a Subchapter "S" corporation?

I'm a small painting contractor. When I checked into becoming an "S" Corporation, they told me I would have to issue stock. Would that be worthwhile? I do the taxes, so I'd like to know how this change would effect my tax status.

■A Sub-chapter "S" corporation - and this is an over simplification - is simply an extension of yourself. For tax purposes you're treated as an individual. For legal purposes, you're treated as a corporation. I am surprised that your accountant did not make you a Sub "S" to begin with. Issuing the stock is just a paper transaction, there is nothing to that.

You ought to stick to painting houses and let the accountant do your taxes. How can you keep up with the tax laws? In my opinion, you need higher experts. I would not consider filling out a tax form myself.

CHAPTER 2 *Insurance*

> **" A million dollars sounds like a lot of insurance, but it's not. You could cause a million dollars worth of grief. "**

Shouldn't we insure our house for the full market value?

Our insurance company sent us a notice that we were over-insured. There's a $32,000 difference between what we paid for the house and what they insured us for. I wanted to carry a policy worth the full amount.

■That's not right. When was the last time you saw a lot burn up? You do not insure the lot, there just is no need to. There is no point insuring a house for a million if it is only worth $100,000, because you cannot collect more than $100,000.

Is our home adequately insured?

We purchased our home about twenty years ago and the insurance company has periodically increased the value of the policy to keep up with the market value of the house, but I'm not so sure I could replace it for its insured value.

■Basically, there are two types of policies you can purchase. One is called a "replacement value" and the other is "fair market value." There is a difference between the two. You can go out and buy a 19th century Victorian house with 18 rooms and all. In some parts of the country you might pay $100,000. That would be the fair market value. But, if you went down to the friendly builder and had him build an 18 room Victorian house, it might cost you a quarter of a million dollars.

You have a choice, when it comes to home insurance. Should you buy a replacement policy? Or should you buy a market value policy? Choosing the replacement policy will cost you more money.

The same principle applies to the contents of the home. If you try to sell your eight year old sofa for what you paid for it, you'll quickly learn what it's worth on the open market. But if it burns up, and you need to replace it, you'll need more than your neighbor would pay you for it at a garage sale. You'll need the money it would cost you to go into a furniture store and buy one like it.

As a mobile home renter do I have to get personal injury insurance?

■Yes, you buy what is called a tenant's form. It is very similar to a home owner's policy except it does not cover the home. Your tenant's policy will pay if you cause injury or damage to someone while they are in your home. Since you are the tenant you are responsible for that.

If there's a fire you will recover the value of your goods, but not the value of the dwelling itself, since you have no interest in that. You're covered in the event of a burglary.

The tenant's form is a package policy that includes all these separate coverages.

Should adding an umbrella policy double our insurance rates?

I want to raise the coverage on our car from its current $25,000, which I know is way too low. The agent said before they can issue an umbrella policy I first had to raise my auto coverage to $500,000. The premium would be at least double what I'm paying now. Then the umbrella addition would cost approximately $420. I have a spotless driving record. I asked for someone to come out and talk with me, but they only do business by mail.

■I would look around a little bit. In my opinion you are being way overpriced. With only $25,000 coverage you have been improperly insured. You have a poor insurance agent.

You do have to separate the level of coverage on your car with the total umbrella coverage. When you're shopping for rates, keep that in mind. $300,000 dollar coverage on your car will cost you one amount and an umbrella policy to cover total liability - house, car, whatever will be issued at a separate rate.

I would not consider doing business with a company that did not have living, breathing people to call on. I'm not telling you to go out and cancel anything, just investigate the market place.

Am I over-insured?

I used to have only $25,000 insurance on my car. I called my company and had it raised to $100,000. My husband tells me it is a waste of money because the person who would not settle for $25,000 is still going to sue us if we have $100,000.

■Only $25,000 car insurance is insane. You are grossly under in-sured. And $100,000 will pay off a lot more things than $25,000. Your husband is wrong.

Do I need a million dollars worth of insurance coverage?

I have $100,000 - $300,000 insurance on my car. I am 38 years old with a perfect driving record.

■Your driving record does not make you immune from a serious accident. A million dollars sounds like a lot of insurance, but it's not. You could cause a million dollars worth of grief. In this day and age, it's possible for anyone to be vulnerable to some heavy litigation.

The point is, if you caused a million dollars worth of damage, you would want enough money to put things as right as dollars can put things. When you raise your car policy I would also elevate your home owner's or renters policy. I'm talking about an umbrella policy.

Can someone successfully sue for an injury after five years?

A customer in my beauty salon poured herself a cup of coffee. She dropped the pot and cut herself. After five years I received notice that she is suing me. Do you think she has a case?

■If she had brought a prompt action, the chances are your insurance company would have paid her something. But most jurisdictions have a three year statutory period during which one must initiate a proceeding. That does not mean that you have to settle in that amount of time, but you have to initiate the suit.

You have been robbed of your defense, because during the time that has passed, you had no notion that there was going to be a lawsuit. Witnesses have disappeared. I would doubt if this would be a serious matter. Do not worry about it, that is what insurance is all about.

Should I sue the party that ran into me for the deductible on my policy?

They ran into my parked car and admitted guilt. My insurance company will waive the deductible if I'm not at fault. But, because I waited four months to report the accident, they said they cannot recover now. They are ready to give me a check for the damages, minus the deductible.

■When you take the money from your company, you give up the right to sue for the physical damage. You have a choice to make. I cannot make the decision for you. There is no guarantee that you are going to collect from the other guy in a law suit. You say you are right and you may have to prove it in court and that may take a couple of years.

I do not see why they cannot recover after four months. But let's clarify something here about "waiving the deductible," as you put it. If you have collision insurance, you have an option. You can collect from your own company, less the deductible amount, or they can bring an action against the guy who did damage to you. They may or may not be successful in collecting from him. That means they may not get enough to give you back your deductible.

The other scenario is to bring an action or claim against the other party and if their company decides that you are right and their guy is wrong, then a judgment is arrived at. Now, those are the two basic decisions that have to be made. It is not a question of waiving the deductible. They will try to collect it from the other party. There is a big difference between the two things.

Should we have trip insurance for a cruise we're taking?

My husband, my mother-in-law and I are going to Alaska in the summer. The total price for the cruise will be $6,000 and the trip insurance for all of us will be about $400. I'm 61 and my husband is 62. We are in good health. The only problem is his mother. She is not doing too well.

■If everybody is healthy and other things are equal, I would say no on the insurance. But you are telling me that there is something in your life that is unstable and I would want to be absolutely certain that that possibility was covered by the insurance. Right now you don't know if it is. There is no point in speculating - I suggest you find out if it covers difficulties that extend to other members of your family.

Covering $6,000 with a $400 premium is a very substantial rate - something on the order of 4%. But, if you are really concerned about your in-law's health, and that is covered, then I would go ahead and get the insurance. You'll feel better about the whole thing and you will not be sitting around sweating your $6,000 in three or four months. Piece of mind has a value.

Are we liable for injuries to neighborhood kids who play on property we rent to someone?

Every summer we rent out half of our property to a circus family. They put up a trapeze for practice and some kids came to play on it. We have release forms signed by their parents and our tenants. Does that absolve us of responsibility?

■The releases are worthless. The answer is for you to insist that your tenants get an insurance policy which names you as a co-insured for enough money to cover any problems that might exist or develop. Then I want you to call the insurance broker to make certain that the policy is in force.

How do I find a good disability insurance company?

I've been shopping around, talking to brokers, and most of them seem to be trainees, or they push one particular company.

■I would never try and select an insurance company myself. You've got to find a competent broker. Let him do that. It's what he gets paid for.

I had lunch with my broker the other day, who is also a good friend, and we discussed my various polices. I keep him for a good reason - he takes very good care of me. Whatever type of insurance I'm looking for, he will shop the marketplace for the best coverage. He will put the facts in front of me. If I have a claim he is the only guy I want to talk to. He is the one who talks to the adjuster and he negotiates for me. I do not have time for that stuff, furthermore, I don't have the expertise. And you probably don't either.

Do church board members need liability insurance?

Also, how vulnerable is the church? We rent out a building we own for other community functions. Our clergymen give counseling. Some of our trustees say that since we are doing a good thing in the community, nobody would ever sue us.

■If your insurance policy doesn't specifically spell out that you rent out the building, you are in jeopardy in my view. Your best friends, your children, your parents, your lover, will sue you under the right conditions.

You should be carrying a director's insurance policy. The members who said nobody would sue are the very ones who are going to get sued. You sue the board of directors individually. You sue everybody in sight. Then hopefully everybody in sight gets excused. But in the meantime, it costs money to get excused.

Without the appropriate insurance in place you are being extremely foolish staying in that position. If the others want to keep their heads in the sand, that's their problem.

There is a chance that your personal liability coverage would protect you, but that is a question for your insurance broker or agent. If he says it does cover you, I would get the opinion in writing.

Say somebody comes in there and falls down, breaks their neck and becomes paralyzed and you are judged legally responsible. Don't you think you are morally responsible to have the assets to meet the obligation?

Can I sue because of a fall down the stairs at our apartment?

I live with my boyfriend and I recently fell down the stairs to our apartment. My wrist is fractured and my arm's in a cast. If I file a claim, would it be what they call a "nuisance claim"?

■The question is - was anybody liable? There is no question about your being injured, but I don't know who you'd bring suit against unless you sue your boyfriend. But since you are a resident of that property there may be medical coverage that you could collect under, rather than on the liability portion. Medical pays without regard to liability. Whether it covers a resident of the property or not is something you'd have to determine.

A "nuisance claim" is when the insurance company gives you, for example, a thousand dollars to drop your suit because it would cost them more than that to defend the issue. What that has done is encourage all kinds of frivolous litigation. But insurance companies are starting to say no to nuisance claims. If a claim has no merit, they're willing to spend $2000 so they don't have to pay out $500, figuring eventually it will turn people off from making these kinds of claims.

Can our home owner's policy be canceled just because our dog bit someone?

We're being sued by a meter reader for $3,000.

■Of course it can be cancelled. Your insurance company is nervous about a dog that bites, and in most states there is no defense. A dog is always wrong unless it is on a leash. If you are out there with your dog and someone comes up and rapes you and the dog bites the rapist, the dog is wrong. But if the rapist kicks the dog, then the dog can defend himself.

CHAPTER 3 *Personal*

" My advice to you is be an activist - somebody who goes out and says...okay, we are going to make an example of a politician. "

Where can I find counseling on handling personal finances?

I am getting married shortly and I'd like to know how to prepare myself. Should I go to our church, or a marriage counselor?

■I think the community college level is the best place to look. I don't think you are looking for marriage or religious counseling. It sounds like you see some deficiencies in your financial training, budgeting, that sort of thing. If you don't know how to set up a budget, there are any number of places you can get help on that, but start with your community college.

Can my former girlfriend prevent me from helping to support our child?

I want to help but she doesn't want the support money. And, if she doesn't want it now, can she come back later and demand it?

■Maybe she can. There is no way to protect yourself. The child is yours. If she changes her mind, you may have to come up with it. I do not think you can force her to take the support if she doesn't want it. And, if you want to visit the child, you may have to get an attorney and go to court.

How can I get financial assistance for the care of my son?

He was seriously injured in a fire. Medicaid will take care of him in the nursing facility but not at home and that's where I'd like him to be. He lived in a special handicapped apartment building. We believe that negligence came into play - the alarm was cut off after he had cried for help.

■If there is negligence, You should talk to an attorney. This is a very difficult situation. I think perhaps you may be wise to allow him to stay in a nursing home setting for a little while until the dust settles. This way he will receive the type of care he requires and it will allow you to have the opportunity to visit with him as much as possible.

I applaud the fact that you are willing to take him into your home. The responsibility could be great.

What can I do to bring justice to two juvenile boys who raped my 14 year old daughter?

One boy is 17, the other is 16. The court gave each of them just 120 days probation. The stiffest punishment is six months incarceration. I talked to the head of the Juvenile Justice Department, the Attorney General's office, and the Minnesota Crime Office. The result - a big fat zero. And these boys were already on probation - one boy has done this to two other girls that I've talked with. We were advised against having them tried as adults, because it would be a jury trial and the emotional distress for my daughter would not be worth it. I know people who have stolen things and been put in jail for nine months. There are just no guidelines. I told every official I talked to that the system raped us all over again.

■I have no way to disagree with you. It's an imperfect system. My advice to you is become an activist - somebody who goes out and says...okay, we are going to make an example of a politician. I'm going to work to replace him or her with somebody who thinks as I do. If you think I am just beating a hollow drum, that's why I got involved in politics many years ago. I got angry at the way things in my town were being run, so I took a shot at running it myself.

I hear people ask, "What can I do, I'm just a little peon." Well, little peons vote don't they? The next election, get as many moms together as possible and run this judge right out of office. You will send a clear and strong message, "If you don't punish people like this, we will run you out of office too." They may just get the message.

We are the people who elect judges. Some judges are very liberal in their interpretation of the law - those that believe perpetrators should be let go to rehabilitate themselves. On the other side are the Roy Bean's of the world whose one choice is to hang them. But most judges fall somewhere in the middle. As a parent, I can appreciate and share your rage at the judge who would not provide what we would believe is justice. But I am afraid that's the system. So, use it.

94% of all incumbents get re-elected. They know they can spit right in the milk and it's not going to bother anybody in the slightest. Stop thinking of yourself as a peon and think of yourself as an activist. Until you do there is really not much hope for any of us, is there?

As parents we might have a difficult time explaining it to our kids. We try to tell them, trust in the law. Obey the law and if you have a problem, see a cop and so on and so forth. And then something of this nature happens and you get some jurist who decides it's not going to do any good to put these kids away. At 17 you're old enough to join the army and shoot at people. I love the expression, "the poor youth." The "youth" is 6 foot 6 and weighs 290 lbs. I think kids ought to be tried as adults, if for only one reason, to set an example for other kids. Because these kids will go back and brag about what they did.

I know it hurts, but there's nothing you can do about those boys. They have been exonerated. That business is over. But you might be able to change the course of history for some other little girl.

How can I locate a child I gave up for adoption twenty six years ago?

I think she has a right to know me. I know where she was born, and I know where her family resided because this was a private adoption through a doctor and an attorney. I have papers from the Alma Organization and the name of the doctor in the city where she was born.

■There are a couple of organizations that are devoted to bringing people together or at least giving them an option to come together and they are very helpful in sorting these types of things out. They have developed techniques for locating people.

Contact the doctor. He or she may not be under any obligation to tell you anything. Contact the attorney who arranged the adoption.

A caution - you do not know if your daughter knows she is adopted. I would not want to be the one to walk up 26 years into her life and tell her that she was adopted. An attorney could contact her, informing her that if she wished to meet her natural mother, she should contact him. It is a very delicate matter. The attorney probably could counsel you on the best approach.

How can I get my girlfriend to go steady with me again?

I'm 14 and I have been going out with this girl for about a month. I found out that she was going out with someone else and I was not even told. I really like her a lot.

■You are too young to go steady. You should be playing the field. I mean, come on man, there is a huge menu out there. You should go for the entire works.

There's no reason why you can't like her. But that doesn't mean you can't go out and find someone else and take them out. Maybe she did the right thing.

For whatever it is worth I think, at your age, you would be a whole lot better off to go out and date other girls and when she sees you walking to the next ball game or whatever with another girl, she will think about that a little bit. And if you never go out again, don't worry about it. Go for the different flavors, not just one. Hang in there, son.

CHAPTER 4 *Real Estate*

" The idea of paying off a mortgage early is a good idea and a bad idea. "

How do I find a good real estate attorney?

I have been ripped off a couple times during the escrow process. They told me that there were no taxes owed on the property that I was buying. Two years down the road I found out otherwise and there's no way I can find the previous owner. Then I discovered that the taxes are on the property - not on the person.

■Find a good general practitioner to handle it. I would want an attorney to represent me in every real estate transaction coming or going. I want somebody to check it out thoroughly. If your attorney screws up, you can take an action against him.

How do I know if I'm getting a good deal on the house I'd like to buy?

It was listed at $120,000. The owner said he would sell for $92,000 and he settled for $88,000. I've called realtors and asked what replacement values are for a house this size. Their numbers come out to about what I'm paying. My two concerns are that real estate is a little soft in this area and it is a little bit more house than the wife and I need. I'm 30 and my job situation is pretty solid.

■Checking with the realtors doesn't tell you too much. It simply says you are paying about what the market will bear. Whether it is a good deal or not is a different matter.

Real estate is worth only what a willing buyer and willing seller agree on. Replacement costs are a whole different thing. It is unlikely that you can replace this house for what you are going to pay for it. But, on the other side of that, you can buy thirty five other houses in your area that you couldn't replace at that price. So that in itself doesn't make it a great deal. What you are looking for is to be able to buy it for less than the going market price in your area.

There are so many other variables, of course. The proximity of a highway could either make or break the value of a house. How far is it from the school? How much traffic is there on the street? Do you have a couple of neighbors who can make life miserable?

The house should be thoroughly inspected - plumbing, roof, foundation etc. Make sure all the i's are dotted and the t's crossed. Make sure the financing is something you can live with.

There is very little doubt in my mind that sooner or later property values are going to recover in your area. I would take advantage of that situation if I were you. You're young and your family will grow, so the fact that the house is larger than you need now is not really a negative.

Why would a seller want to back out of a deal if the FHA doesn't appraise the house for the selling price?

■He doesn't want the FHA to come back and say the house is worth a thousand dollars less than the selling price. If that happened he'd have to reduce his price in order for you to qualify for financing. Backing out on someihing like this is not unreasonable from his point of view.

Is it feasible to use a land contract as collateral in purchasing a piece of property?

I realize I would have to discount it. What would be a reasonable percentage? Is it worth pursuing?

■I would think it is a great collateral item, unless it is an extraordinarily valuable property and the difference between what is owed and what the property is worth is significant. It also depends upon whether or not the potential lender feels your collateral is solid.

The amount you will have to discount depends upon the value of the property, the strength of the person on the other end of this contract and how well the contract was written. Where the property is located is also important because the strength of land contracts varies from state to state.

Is now a good time to buy a home?

I am 38 years old, single, and I make $16,700 a year. I can't pay more than $34,000. My dad said he would help me with the down payment. I've thought about a condo, but I don't like having to pay a maintenance fee on top of the monthly payment.

■You are a prime candidate for a condo. I understand your view of maintenance fees. But, in a traditional single family home, you've got taxes to pay and all the stuff to fix and paint. The maintenance fee on the condo takes care of the exterior maintenance. It does not really matter what you call it, as long as the total number of dollars going out stays within the norm you have established.

Also, with a condo, you are buying a little different lifestyle. If you don't like all the mickey mouse cutting of grass and whatever, the condo lifestyle could be much more to your liking and your temperment.

Oh sure, it may not be the house of your dreams, but you have to creep before you crawl. You work up to these things. You should have started this ten years ago, but the longest journey begins with one step and it seems like today is the day to take it.

What is the rule of thumb in deciding how big a mortgage you can take on?

My husband and I are in our late 20's, both working, bringing in about $30,000 combined.

■Double your annual income is not a bad guideline for the average person. In your case that's a $50,000-$60,000 house. If you can do better than that, do it.

Other things to consider are your lifestyle, the stability of your income, how much you are prepared to sacrifice toward a dwelling unit.

There is another thing that you may want to consider. Maybe buy a multiple home. A duplex. That way you will have some help - the rent you collect will help pay your mortgage. You will be able to buy a more expensive property with no more money or perhaps less coming out of your pocket and, at the same time, you'll be building equity on a more substantial property.

Is it true that you are only allowed to use a VA loan one time?

■No, that is not true. Once the VA loan has been satisfied - paid off - then you can re-apply for a new certificate of eligibility. Although I don't believe that holds true for an assumable loan.

Should I refinance my home?

I have a 12% mortgage now through a private party with payments of about $660 a month. I can get a 7 3/4% adjustable rate mortgage for 30 years and lower my payment to $400 a month. If I do that, should I put the money I save back into paying off the mortgage?

■Here are some questions you should get answers to: How long does it stay at 7 3/4? A year? Two? Six months? What is the rate tied to? Treasury bills? Federal Fund rate? How much can it vary?

As to whether you should put the extra money into paying off the house sooner, well, that depends. If we go back to 1979 when 21% interest rates were common, you wouldn't pay off a nickel off before you had to because you could invest it elsewhere and make a terrific return on your money. On the other side of that if the best return you can get, with the kind of safety you are looking for, is maybe 8%, obviously you would pay the mortgage down.

Is there a formula to use when looking for residential rental property to invest in?

I am making a trade. I owned a piece of property that I bought for a certain amount per acre and realized the profit on it and I did not want to pay the taxes. I have to make a quick decision within forty-five days.

■There are number of ways you can look at it. It depends on the cost of your money - paying 8% for money is a whole different thing than paying 18%. The neighborhood is another factor. Is it declining or is it booming?

There are also the personal questions. Do you want the income now or do you want to postpone it? Are you interested in appreciation or depreciation with regard to taxes? Also, because of tax laws, there are many variables in regards to managing it. Until you establish what you want from this investment, you cannot decide what property to buy.

On balance, I would like to have my debt serviced and reasonable return on my capital. What the depreciation is worth depends upon your tax situation. The most important thing to me is the potential for substantial appreciation.

On a trade, you do not obviate any taxes, you postpone them. There is a big difference. You are going to pay the taxes eventually. The rationale for postponing is that later may be a better time to pay taxes and you have use of the money for about ten years.

Can I sell my house without a broker?

I've been advertising for about eight months. I've gotten a few nibbles, but the market is not good here. I don't want to give up and call a broker and give them six or seven percent. I feel I can handle all the broker's functions - purchase agreements, helping with financing, etc., but I do not have access to the leads. I'm trying to evaluate what that is worth. Should I pay 7% for leads?

■Let's start with this premise: brokers earn their money. That does not mean that you cannot sell a piece of property by yourself. But there are a number of things that you will have to do.

You will have to know a little bit about pricing the house. I suspect that is your biggest problem - your house is overpriced. If it has been on the market for eight months and has not sold, it is overpriced. That doesn't mean it's not worth what you are asking - it might cost twice that much to replace it, you may have paid more than that, etc., - but a piece of property is only worth what a buyer is willing to pay, and a seller is willing to accept. That is one function a broker performs, along with pre-qualifying buyers.

Before showing the property, a good broker will qualify the potential buyers. That way he doesn't waste anyone's time by showing them a piece of property they can't afford. That's one more thing you have to do if you are going to sell your property yourself.

Obviously, the broker is paying for his leads by maintaining an office and a staff, advertising, and being available seven days a week. Whether those leads are worth 7% is a matter that is difficult to determine. You have not been doing so good on your own.

Brokers earn every penny that they are paid. If you take on their task you have to give up a good deal. As an example you have to be around on weekends. You have to know how much to charge, based on what's selling or not selling in your area. You have to have access to the financing and establish contacts. There are a lot of reasons why it is smart to use a broker, but there is no reason in the world why you cannot attempt to do it yourself. If it doesn't work out, go to a professional.

Would it be better to wait three weeks to receive title to my home, or take a quitclaim?

We paid off a home loan three months ago. I have a cancelled check. My problem is that I cannot get my title. They keep telling me that in a couple of weeks they'll get back to me. I called today and was told that the clerk had called the courthouse and had learned that the abstract title was clear. They offered to mail me an application for a quitclaim deed. If you were in my shoes, would you want that?

■I would get some legal help. I am not sure that a quitclaim is what we are looking for here. You paid off the mortgage and you want a satisfaction of lien.

I would have an attorney determine exactly what the status of your lien is now. I do not know what the law is in your state to accomplish what we are trying to do here. There may be a way to have this done through some state authority. Your attorney should know.

Get the satisfaction filed. Do not sit on it. The quicker the better. Ask him or her to sit down with you and outline the situation and a plan. If the savings and loan has a bigger problem, you could be caught up in the mess.

How important is it for me to hire a building inspector and an attorney?

I am buying a new condo for $115,000 from a very reputable builder who has three such developments under his belt. The only problem that I could see arising would be in the figures, as to whether they are correct or not. An attorney friend agrees and told me to get the closing papers to him a couple of days in advance and he would read them.

■In the first place, the fact that the condo is new or used is relevant, because I would not pay for an inspector on a brand new building. New properties have certain guarantees. Regarding the attorney, it doesn't matter whether it's 100 years old or is being built as we speak, you need representation.

If all your friend, the attorney, is going to do is read them and send you on your way, you have a less than competent attorney in my view. You're spending $115,000 and somebody tells you not to spend $400 for an attorney? Does that make any kind of sense? That amount, by the way, is deductible against the gain when you sell it.

I challenge the average person to understand what they are signing when they buy real estate. It is a complex procedure. You are depending on somebody's integrity. I'm a firm believer in experts. I want to depend on someone who is an expert, who is there with only one person's interest at heart - mine. And, I want that person to understand if they screw up, I'll come after them legally.

A general practitioner should be able to handle it for you. If he can't, he ought to tell you.

How do I go about trading a house, rather than selling it?

A friend worked out a three way trade on his property and it sounded interesting. I wondered if it could work for me. I bought a house eight years ago and it's value has doubled in that time. I'd like to sell it, but I don't want to have to pay the taxes on the profit.

■Here's how a three way trade works. You see a piece of property you want. You have to buy it with something, so you tell the seller of that property he must take your property in trade for his. Then you arrange for a sale of that property to a third party. All we are doing is shuffling paper around. If you do it the way I described, as long as the property you buy is worth as much or more than the property that you are getting rid of, it is not a taxable event.

If and when you want to cash out - sell the house outright and take the money and run - you have to pay the taxes. The chicken will have just came home to roost.

Which is a better investment - multiple or single family dwellings?

I am considering the option of buying an apartment building. But I'm wondering if I should consider looking for better individual deals in single family units in the area?

■To tell you the truth, I think multi-family is easier than single. I really do. You are focused on one area instead of scattered all over. You confine your problems to one place, instead of all over town. Secondly, the problems are diminished to the extent that you have one roof over ten people instead of ten different roofs to worry about. The same thing is true with groundskeeping and all that sort of stuff.

Your dollar goes a lot further too. Your cost per unit is usually significantly lower. I am not sure that I would go into apartments. I think two or three family units are the way to go. They are more manageable and do not have as many regulations.

How can I be sure that a house awarded to me in a divorce settlement will be transferred without liens against it?

My husband left the state leaving behind a trail of bills. He probably owes $50,000. The house may be worth $80,000.

■There is no way the house will come to you without liens being satisfied. You will have to pay them before the house is signed over to you.

If there are liens of $50,000 plus the mortgage, there apparently is nothing left for you. The house is not going to come to you. You are better off to walk away from it.

But before you consider anything, it would be wise to verify what liens have actually been placed against the house. Go to the county courthouse and find out immediately. If all his debtors have filed liens against the house, for all intents and purposes, there is no house.

If there are no liens other than the mortgage, then you may want to consider selling the place. That will require his signature unless he has already quitclaimed it to you.

Am I liable to pay for repairs on a house that I sold three months ago?

The buyer says they spent $2,000 dollars to take care of damp-ness in the basement. Prior to the sale, they called in an inspector and there was no evidence of moisture in the basement. I have an attorney now, but I did not have one representing me at the sale.

■The new owners should be looking to the inspector, not you. In certain states, where there are disclosure laws, it is required that if you know of a deficiency, you have to disclose it. In every situation that I know of, if someone asks you, "Do you have ants?", and you lie, you have made a misrepresentation.

Because you weren't represented by an attorney, you might have to spend more money defending this action. If you were represented at the closing, the attorney would have already deter-mined if any representations were made. You cannot prevent anyone from suing you.

I would have my attorney call their guy and tell him to stop rattl-ing my client's cage and go after the inspector.

Should I try to sell my mobile home for less than I owe, and take a loss?

It's been on the market for several months. It's in a mobile home park and some people tell me that's part of the problem. I don't want to go through the trouble of moving it. I'm asking $30,000, which is what I owe on it. I paid $34,000 for it three years ago.

■It must be a function of price. I suspect that you picked the price predicated on what you owe. That is not necessarily a valid way to fix a price. Apparently, it is not worth that much.

It would appear that it is not worth $30,000, because if it was, someone would have bought it for $30,000. You can buy a pretty nice condo for $30,000 in some parts of the country. You are competing for the housing dollar.

You should be pricing other mobile homes. See what other people are asking and getting.

Should I default on a mobile home mortgage to get out from under the obligation?

I have consulted an attorney who advises me to write to the credit company, telling them that I intend to default on the loan. He said they will sell the trailer and sue me for the difference between what I owe and what they received from the sale. He also advised me to declare bankruptcy so that the bank could not collect the money from me. I am 27 years old and earn $30,000 a year. I have no other debts. Would this be a good idea? I can't seem to sell it for what I owe on it - $24,000.

■The defaulting procedure is called a deficiency. I think he is correct. They will do that.

As for the bankruptcy idea, I think he has seriously ill-advised you. If worse came to worse, I think you would sell the trailer for $19,000. You have to grow up and take your loss. The last thing you need is a bankruptcy in your background for $5,000. To go bankrupt for one-sixth of your annual income is a tragedy.

Bankruptcy can stay with you for ten years and, as a practical matter, it will stay with you for life. You wouldn't want that for $5,000. It really distresses me that an attorney would give that kind of advice, particularly to a young person like yourself.

You will have to keep lowering the price until it sells or try to rent it to somebody.

How can I be certain a house I'm buying is not settling?

What concerns me is that the basement has a poured concrete floor with cinder block walls. If you look where the wall meets the floor, you see that there's about a one-inch gap. I do not know if this indicates some kind of bad settling or that the walls are shifting outward away from the house.

■It is really counter productive for me to speculate. Wouldn't it make good sense to put $250 into a home inspection?

If I were buying this home, I would have it inspected by a professional. He or she will call a problem like that to your attention and tell you what the consequences are - what you have to look forward to in the way of cost to correct the problem, whatever it may be.

I would want someone who knows the construction business. More importantly, it should be someone familiar with your area. They would know the soil conditions, etc. These are things that a local construction professional would know.

How can I get a mortgage holder to compromise on a pay-back arrangement?

I made an agreement to bring my house payments up to date again. I've been behind for about a year. I would pay $1,000 a week for the first four weeks and make a $7,000 payment the fifth week. That would bring me current. I've made four weekly payments, but I cannot make the fifth $7,000 payment. I want to offer to continue with the $1,000 a week arrangement until I'm paid up. The person in the collection department said no.

■You are in default and they are holding the cards, but I think they are very foolish. You ought to make an appointment with one of the major officers.

For the lower level guy, there is no incentive to go along with you. I really can't fault them because they are doing what they are told and there is no advantage for them to stick their neck out for you. That's why you have to deal with someone at the top level. If they have a brain, they are going to realize that they are on the hook and certainly don't want to go through a foreclosure, if they can avoid it. You will be current in five or six weeks, they should give you a shot.

How can I get my real estate deposit back?

We did not qualify for a mortgage on a house that we agreed to buy. The deposit is being held by the seller's real estate agent in an escrow account. They are holding about $6,000 and asking for damages. Our lawyer can't get the seller to sign the release of funds.

■I am sure your contract clearly states that if financing is not available the deal is off, otherwise your attorney who let you sign a deal would have to have a screw loose. It clearly says that if a mortgage is not obtained each party's responsibility ends and all monies will be returned.

If you can't get their cooperation, you'll need to go to court. I cannot look into a judge's heart, but I think the court would order the real estate agent to release the escrow funds. He cannot put that house back on the market until he resolves the whole thing. As a matter of fact, you can move to have the house tied up until this is resolved. I think I would do that as a little defense mechanism.

Should I build a house on spec?

I was thinking about building and moving into the house until I sell it. There's just me and my wife and it seems feasible. I have worked in various facets of the construction industry, so I have some experience as a craftsman. We've considered buying a place to renovate, but the sellers I've talked to are figuring what it is going to be worth when it is done and subtracting how much they think it is going to cost to fix it up and selling it for that figure. There's no profit.

■I am not comfortable with building houses on speculation. I want to have the house sold before I take the first shovel-full of dirt out of the ground. If you can get a sales contract before you build, then you can zing right through the entire transaction. You push like crazy because you get your money as soon as the thing is done. When you build on spec, you have nothing to sell until it the house is half way up.

Of course it is feasible. The area in which you are building has a great deal to do with your decision to build or not to build. If the market's soft, a person would be foolish to build a house, whether it's on spec or just to live in. The reason is that the cost per square foot of building is not influenced very much by the economic conditions of the area. It could cost you just as much to build in a depressed area as it does in a thriving area. In a slow or soft market, you can go out and buy an existing house for less money. In some places it may be cheaper to build property.

If things are really swinging in an area, it's a seller's market. Stuff goes on the market today and is sold tomorrow. In that case it may pay you to build.

Let me tell you something. Building is a master undertaking. I believe the majority of people would say they would not do it again. There are a lot of headaches.

You may have worked in the craft area. That's easy compared to more difficult transactions, such as getting through the various codes, financing and insurance tangles. You have to depend on subcontractors for the things you can't do yourself. You have to buy materials and make certain that you don't have any mechanics liens, etc. Bringing all these things together is a full time job.

I am not so sure how long your wife will put up with moving in and moving out. If I were going to do what you are describing, I would renovate. Buy homes that are beat up. You may not find the perfect deal right out of the chute. That is not to say that those homes do not exist. People die and estates want settle in a hurry, etc. They're not easy to find, but I think you are far better off doing that than trying to move into a house you are building.

Do I have any recourse against a builder who did not complete construction when he promised?

The city inspected the house and passed it, but the gas lines were not in. In the meantime, the builder had told me to go ahead and give notice to my landlord. I cannot occupy the house and I have to be out of my apartment. The gas company said that they would go ahead and put in the line, but it would take six weeks.

■The city is responsible to some degree, because you relied on their inspection and they should not have passed it if the gas service wasn't in.

Why don't you move in and, if necessary both your stove and hot water heater can be converted to bottled gas temporarily. I would go to the builder for any extra expenses involved.

I cannot imagine how the city could okay the inspection without the appropriate utilities being connected and inspected. If you had an attorney, he ought to be reprimanded because that is one of the things you ask for before you close. The escrow company is not going to ask about that. So, the lesson is - hire an attorney for any real estate transaction!

What's the best way to straighten out a mistake in a utility bill?

I was on vacation for a month. I turned off the water heater and the furnace and there is no pilot on the stove. My meter shows I used gas. My bill came and it's $30.00. A typical monthly bill is about $100.00.

■There are a couple of possibilities here. One is that there was a bad reading. The second possibility is that you had an estimated bill. You should look on the statement to see whether it was a reading or an estimated charge. If it was estimated, then the answer is that they did not know you were away, so they continued the estimated consumption. I have never heard of a utility cheating anybody.

It's a mistake, by the way, to turn off the water heater. It is very hard on the unit to shut it off and turn it on again.

Will a new mall near a house raise or lower my property value?

I am hoping to buy a house right next to where they are building a shopping center.

■It could be either one. If you are in an area where the traffic coming directly to and from the mall will spill over on residential streets, that could hurt you. On the other side if you are close to the mall and yet insulated from it, which is possible, then your property values could go up.

If I sell my house and let someone assume the first, am I on the hook if they don't make the payments?

I heard about a lady who let the buyers assume her VA loan. They defaulted, but she didn't find out until she drove by the house and saw it was vacant. She was surprised also to learn that she couldn't get her house back. Couldn't she step in, pay the house payment and resell the house?

■You are still on the hook. The lady you're talking about was still on the bond and because she didn't know the loan was in default, it went to foreclosure. I don't believe she could get the house back, it would be sold at auction. She is still on the hook.

On an assumption, the trick is to get enough equity. For example, let's talk numbers here for a moment. Let's say your house is worth $60,000 and the mortgage the buyer is assuming is $28,000. In that case, there is nothing to worry about because there is $32,000 worth of equity. If there is a foreclosure, there is going to be a sale. With the numbers I mentioned, there will be more than enough money generated at sale to pay off the mortgage. If the mortgage is paid off, the seller is off the hook. On the other hand, if the mortgage was $50,000 and the house was worth $52,000, you could get yourself in trouble. The house could easily sell for less than what's owed on it. If they elected to go after you, they could.

A lot of people do not know what they are getting themselves into with assumptions. Also, if your buyer defaults, it shows on your credit rating. As I said, there is safety in numbers - the down payment.

This is hearsay, okay, but I understand that the VA has not been actively pursuing these matters until recently. But, because they have been burned so badly in so many soft real estate markets, they have been obliged to go after people.

Should we pay off the small balance on our existing first mortgage with a home equity loan?

We are adding a room to our house at a cost of about $14,000. We have about $11,000 left on the original home loan. The interest rate on that is 6%. The lender recommended combining the two and getting a Home Equity Loan. We are trying to keep the monthly payments down.

■The lender gave you poor advice. I would not get rid of the 6% mortgage. And I would not pay cash because you will lose what little tax advantage that is left to you. I would get a Home Equity Loan for the $14,000 at the best price I could get.

Let's say you get the money for 11%. Why would you get rid of the first mortgage at 6%, so you have the privilege of paying 11%? Does that make any sense? I believe the guy is blowing smoke in your face.

Keeping the monthly payments down is one thing, but there is no sense in paying double the interest to spread it over a longer period of time.

Should I go with a lease purchase or contract for deed? Or should I wait for a house I can buy outright?

I'm looking at a house with a new FHA loan that the realtors tell me cannot be assumed for two years. What they propose is that I either go with a lease or contract. The seller wants $7,000 down in either case. The price is $69,000. I am wondering, in two years, could FHA turn me down, making it impossible to assume the loan? I earn $27,500 annually.

■If you put $7,000 down, by all means, go for the contract for deed. You know I am not very enthusiastic about contract for deeds, but I would go for that, providing you get the best real estate attorney you can find. He can't protect you totally, but he can wrap it up as tightly as possible. If you really think this is a good deal and that house is in good shape, I'd feel more comfortable with a contract-for-deed than I would with a lease option.

My guess is the rules would not change in two years regarding assumptions. Providing the real estate market in your area is in pretty good shape, I don't think you should pass on it. You should be able to qualify for a $50,000 mortgage without any trouble.

Can I get the credit check fee returned after a loan was denied for other than credit reasons?

I gave them $400 for a credit check, appraisal fee, and various other fees. They said it would take about five or six weeks for closing. So I waited six weeks. Finally, they asked me to bring in the condo association by-laws. A few days later I got a letter saying that the loan was denied because the association wasn't approved. I called another mortgage company and as soon as said condominium, I was told they would send me an application to see if my condominium would qualify. I'm trying to get back my $400.

■I don't think that is going to happen. You have to understand, when you go to a lender, particularly a broker as you did or even your local commercial bank or savings institution, most of these institutions sell your paper on a secondary market. They put it together and then they get paid a servicing fee for collecting the money each month. They sell the mortages to GINNY-MAY, FREDDY-MAY, FREDDY-MAC, etc.

As a consequence, they have to underwrite loans that conform to the underwriting standards of these organizations, so that they can sell them as a group - fifty or a hundred to a package. Frankly I have not heard of the problem you described. The condominium association may have rules that they find are so stringent that it would make the risk on the apartment loan greater.

The lender probably knew the answer as to whether or not the condo association was approved. It would seem to me though, that this problem probably comes up more often in a small condo association than in large one. An astute mortgage broker would have asked the question up front.

Based on all of that, what do you have to lose? I'd go after him. But, you have to have a foundation to go after somebody. I would pick the weakest point in his argument, which is that you went to him as an expert in mortgages, and he should have known that there could be a problem.

What is appropriate for earnest money on a $135,000 house?

Our daughter and son-in-law are trying to buy their first house. The seller wants $4,000 earnest money.

■Anything under 10% would be reasonable - that's $13,500. What I am saying is, if they want to buy this piece of property and they want the seller to draft a contract that says he is going to sell it to them at such and such a price, he needs some serious earnest money.

It is customary to put down 10% of the purchase price upon signing the contract. He has the right to ask whatever he wants. Your daughter has the right to take a hike, saying I don't want to deal with you.

What should I know before I begin investing in income property?

I have always thought about purchasing residential property to rent it out, realizing a positive cash flow. I spent $600 and attended a seminar on the subject and several interesting points were brought out. They talked about things like how a negative cash flow can be good...option buying...and tricky things like that. But I am interested in more straightforward investments. I'm single and 26 years old. I've got about $10,000 to play with.

■I would pick up a two or three-family home. I would pick the apartment that would lend itself most readily to renovation. I would move into that one and fix it up while I lived there. As soon as it was fixed up, I would rent it out, then move the people out of the worst one and move into that one. That's not going to be much fun and you may cramp your social life, but it does lead to a lot of money.

Most of us who have fiddled around with this, including yours truly, have wound up with a negative cash flow and other problems. But, lets look at some top priority consideration before you sink your money into rental property.

You mentioned negative cash flow. It is never good. Like tight shoes, you can put up with them but that doesn't make them comfortable. You're likely to end up with a negative cash flow, if you're in a depressed area where there are an abundance of vacancies and lower rents. So learn about the area.

What happens when the property is vacant for two months and the mortgage company wants their payment? Can you afford to pay them? There's no way to completely protect yourself from that problem. Unless you are sitting in a place like New York, where there are virtually no vacancies, you've got to be concerned about that.

With just $10,000, you are working on a shoe string. You probably have to put 6 or $7,000 down to buy anything. So, if you have a couple of bad months, will you have enough income to pay an extra mortgage payment?

Consider the location in your city. A good spot to be in, is close to a university. There are always kids looking for housing.

Take all that stuff you heard at the seminar with a huge handful of salt.

How can I anticipate where the greatest property appreciation will occur?

I know there are patterns in neighborhoods in larger cities and I want to know how to do the research to allow me to take advantage of those trends. I'm in law school and I'd like to begin building for the future.

■You are making it something entirely too complicated. I think you have it backwards. You're talking about the comeback of the inner cities - it's called centrafication.

You're going to be a law student. I think you are in the right calling, because you can take a simple subject and make it entirely too complicated. Look, all we are talking about is the ability to buy a house on the fringe of an area that you see turning for the better. You don't have to be a genius to predict trends in this regard. All it requires is a lot of hard work.

There are areas, particularly in center cities that are being re-developed, where people are moving back in, spending money, renovating the homes, etc. These homes go up in value. New York City is a huge example, where six years ago brownstone homes were selling for thirty, forty, fifty thousand dollars. Now, those neighborhoods have come back and the same homes are bringing over a million dollars.

What can we do to keep the bank from taking our farm while we try to dig out of trouble?

They're getting ready to take away our family farm. We took out a $250,000 loan to improve production. Since the market has fallen things just aren't so good. We're about eighteen months behind on installments - about $50,000. They are not willing to accept partial payment and they won't consider refinancing. We did find a corporation that's willing to buy it, let us operate it and then sell it back to us at a later date.

■I don't know that you can hold them off. What the bank is saying is, "Look, we loaned you money and under the terms of the loan you have defaulted." The bank is not going to let you dissipate its assets. They are protecting their interests.

I'm not trying to defend the bank, but they are in a bad spot. It looks like a very bad loan on their books. And look at it from the banker's point of view: he has to defend this loan to a bank examiner. That's hard to do. I could be wrong, but I doubt if they are trying to do you out of your farm.

I can understand why that bank is getting a little upset - you are behind a year and a half. The point of negotiation is past. They won't wait for you to sell off 50 or 100 acres to raise some dough. The only other alternative is to try to find money from some other source.

I suppose as a last resort, and maybe you're there, you could go with the corporate buy out - sell back proposition you mentioned. But the interest rates will be huge. I suppose it's a better alternative than none at all, but it is one with which you had better walk very softly. I wish I had a better answer because this is a disease affecting the whole farm belt.

Could the neighbors behind us on a subdivided lot sue for an improper easement?

Several years ago one owner divided his lot in half, front and back, and gave an easement through the front half of the lot to the back half of the lot. Unfortunately, there is no easy way to put in a road without building a bridge. Now the county has come out and said the entire lot cannot be built on.

■The answer is yes they could sue. But this situation is why there is a Board of Adjustments - to get variances on zoning ordinances. No ordinance is perfect or complete. And all zoning ordinances create hardships, and that is what the board of adjustments is there for - to get relief from those hardships.

What the county really said was, the lot was nonconforming. It cannot be built on under terms of the current zoning. But, they could go for a variance, and possibly on a hardship basis, get it. That's all. I don't want to tell you they could or they couldn't. The likelihood is that they could. If there are utilities - sewer, water, that stuff, then they can get an easement for that easily. Then that property probably is still buildable with a variance.

I think the whole thing, to say the least, was sloppy government. The local authorities should never have allowed that kind of a subdivision.

There are no absolutes. What is appropriate today is inappropriate tomorrow, and is appropriate again the following day. Laws are a product of man, and men come and go.

Is it a good idea to pay a mortgage down early?

I have a 30 year mortgage and we have $30,000 to pay at 11.9%. Over the next four years we are anticipating receiving about $7,500 a year. I do have other forms of available liquid cash if needed. I guess I come from the conservative school where you do not like to have a lot of outstanding debts.

■The idea of paying off a mortgage early is a good idea and a bad idea. With an 11.9% mortgage right now, I think the more reasonable thing to do is look at a new mortgage. As these words are being spoken, you could probably get a 3% spread. 3% is well worth it. If you're planning on staying in your house for at least three years, it would pay you to refinance.

When you start talking about 11.9% money and you only get 6% or 7% on your money it obviously makes sense. The problem is that the money is not liquid. If you need the money for a crisis, you cannot get at it. The rejoinder to that is to pay off the mortgage early and apply for a home equity line of credit. Then the money is available if you need cash.

I understand where you are coming from emotionally - saying you do not like having a lot of outstanding debts, and it may be that in your case it pays. But, if I were in your socks, I would be looking for a new mortgage.

" My opinion is that, in this case, you are far better off trying to negotiate than litigate. "

What recourse do we have against a pest control company?

They certified the house several years ago when we moved in and we've been paying them $40 a year on an extended service. They came out for the annual inspection about a month ago and said they saw absolutely nothing. Yesterday we had termites swarming so I called another company who found lots of termite activity and damage to some major beams and floor joists.

■You paid your pest control company as experts. If they did not do their job properly then you have legal recourse. I think clearly there is some responsibility on their part for the damage, otherwise why would you hire them if they were not the experts?

First, I would call the company. Find out what they propose doing. They may tell you they'll make everything right. But if not, and you were represented by an attorney when you purchased your home, call him. He may have been involved in the initial contract with the pest control company. Even if he wasn't, ask him to write a letter since this is an ongoing part of your purchase. But give the company the first shot at making things right.

How can I get money back that my wife took from our joint savings account when we were separated?

I got the proceeds from the sale of our house and put it in the bank. Then we separated. I went to the bank, and there was $64 there instead of $64,000. She says she doesn't have it, but the bank says she drew out that amount.

■A joint account is equal. I have to assume you are suing her for divorce. In your divorce action, you will get credit for that amount of money. It will be part of the community property. The fact that she took it out is evidence that it is, or was, in her custody. It is not necessarily true that money goes from a male to a female. It could go from the female to the male. This will be an issue during the divorce.

What do I do to overturn a condo association rule that I think is in violation of health codes?

The condo association has decided to turn off our kitchen and bathroom exhaust fans every night at 11:00. I have called the Board of Health and they tell me that if there are no windows, you must have use of an exhaust fan twenty four hours a day. What recourse do I have?

■First of all you're wasting your time going around with an empty gun and aiming at people. What you ought to do is find out exactly what the local code says. Find out what the building code requires in that community, not your condo, in the community where you live.

You go get the Code and you find out what specific violation these people are guilty of. Then you make a complaint to the Health Department. Call and tell them that there is a violation in your community ordinance and quote what section it came from. You put the health officer on notice that he has to enforce the ordinance and he will be very happy to do so.

Is it customary for the party bringing a lawsuit to have to pay all court costs?

The attorney forgot to tell us that we have to pay court costs - about $3,000. While I was at work, my fifteen year old daughter was watching the kids. An eight year old neighbor boy shot our twelve year old son with a B-B gun. He lost vision in one eye.

■Your attorney should have informed you up front that the expenses are almost always the province of the litigant... the person bringing the suit. But these expenses can be recovered from the ultimate award - the proceeds coming to you - if you win.

Now, having said that, you must consider your chances for winning. Surely your attorney must have covered this with you. The defense attorney could come after your daughter for not having proper stewardship over your son. I want you to think about this, because it's the kind of stuff they are going to throw at you on the witness stand. If somebody asked you, when you were at work that day, where is Johnny (your son)? What would you have said? With your daughter...right? So, they are probably going to come after her and try to prove that it was her lack of responsibility that contributed to this whole thing. I'm not telling you this to dissuade you from pressing the matter. I'm just telling you what kind of stuff they are going to throw at you.

Given all of that, there is little question in my mind that there will be some kind of recovery. When a child is hurt, insurance companies get very nervous. The last place they want to be is in front of a jury. If you need to borrow the money for costs, you will recoup it from the judgement or settlement.

How do I get a manufacturer to respond to my complaint about being injured by their defective product.

A razor blade split in two while I was using it and I cut myself, leaving three scars on my neck. After two certified letters, I have received no answer from the company. I'm sixty-two years old. I am not after a settlement or anything, but I hate to be ignored over something like this.

■I do not know how you could get their attention unless you want to start a legal action and I don't think you want to do that.

If they have not answered you by now, they are going to stonewall you. They're thinking, "This guy is trying to sue us." A sixty-two year old man doesn't have a prayer of getting compensated for a scar on his neck, in my opinion. If you were a twenty year old woman it would be different.

Can we collect medical bills from a skating rink?

A girl fell in front of our daughter and she tripped over the girl. We talked to a lawyer and he said that we would have to prove negligence - we'd have to prove that the ice was rough. He said he could try sending a letter requesting help with the bills in a spirit of goodwill. He said that is about all the case she would have.

■I do not believe you have much of a case. I think your attorney is right. That is a matter of opinion. The problem is that we have to accept some responsibility for our own actions. She is a big girl, she knew what she was doing, she entered into an activity where there is a certain amount of hazard involved and unfortunately she was one of the people who got hurt. It happens.

Suppose for example, that someone had been complaining for two hours that the ice was in bad shape, perhaps one of their employees dropped something on the ice, creating a hazard. In that case they should shut the place down. That would be negligence on their part. There is nothing negligent about someone falling down and the next person falling over them in a chain reaction. Unfortunately that is the nature of ice skating.

Can I sue a company that dyed my carpet the wrong color?

I hired a carpet cleaning company to dye our light tan carpet brown...Well, now I have purple carpet. And it doesn't go with any of my furniture.

■Yes, but you can't sue for the entire replacement cost. You are not entitled to get more than you had than when you began. So if the rug was, say, five years old, you are entitled to the value of a five year old rug.

If this company holds themselves forth as professionals, they have a responsibility to you to either provide the service that they said they would, or make you whole again.

Can I beat a zoning violation fine for building an airplane in my car port?

A zoning officer cited someone in the neighborhood for junk cars and then cited me for having an aircraft in a residential zone. I enclosed the carport with greenhouse materials and I still had to pay a $550 fine. What can I do?

■If you took the car port and made it into a garage, there is no way they can tell you what to do unless you're making moonshine or cutting coke. But putting greenhouse materials around it is not enclosing.

My personal opinion is I think your zoning officer should have better things to do with his time. So many communities are trying to preserve us from ourselves. I can understand the junk car ordinance. But it's hard to believe they thought about an airplane when they wrote the ordinance. Pragmatically, what you need to do is move and get yourself a garage.

Do I need a lawyer to form a non-profit corporation?

I am a member of a darts organization. We decided that we would like to host a large tournament. In order to get the sponsorship we need, we have to become a non-profit corporation.

■Does a cat have whiskers? Yes, you have to hire an attorney. It would be very foolish to try to do it yourself. You have to conform with the laws of your state regarding the maintenance of a non-profit corporation. You'll have to be apprised of all your responsibilities because they are not insignificant.

For example, in some states a non-profit corporation has to get rid of all its money by the end of the year, with the exception of a few bucks. It can only use the money in certain ways. So get an attorney to very, very carefully explain your responsibilities as well as your privileges and your rights.

How can I collect money from a mail-order company that didn't deliver?

I ordered some banana plants from a company in Michigan. After a few weeks I called and they said I should get my plants at anytime. I waited another couple of weeks and nothing came. Now I just want my $52 back.

■Call the Better Business Bureau in Michigan and make a complaint. Go on record. Then do the same thing in your home town. Unfortunately, when the number of dollars is relatively small, there is only so much you can do before it costs more money than it's worth. On top of that, with such small amounts of money, nobody pays attention. There is very little else you can do.

Selling banana trees in Michigan. That figures. Michigan is noted for its banana industry.

Can I protect the equity in some property from being used up in paying for medical expenses?

The property is owned by our parents and is worth about $150,000. They want it to be be our inheritance. We're thinking of putting the property in someone else's name to protect it, so that if they get sick they won't be able to show any assets and there'll be government help available.

■Given those circumstance do you honestly believe that the government ought to pay your mother's and father's hospital bills even if they are substantial? If your parents don't have medical insurance, why not buy them some. Insure them against catastrophic illness.

If you said you wanted to bury $50,000, no strings attached, I would not have a quarrel. But I really would have a quarrel with someone who has a fair amount of money and buries it in such a way that it makes the rest of us pay the bill.

Should I take a cleaner to small claims court for losing my suits?

They were only six months old and cost me about $325 each. I called him and asked what he was going to do and he offered to pay a total of $250. I think I should get full replacement cost.

■My opinion, for what it is worth, is that you are far better off trying to negotiate than to litigate. Even though you haven't had the suits long - even if they've only hung in the closet for six months - they are probably only worth about half of what you paid for them. That's a total of $350, so you are only $100 apart.

I would give the guy a counter-proposition. Ask him to give you $250 in cash and $100 worth of free cleaning. I wouldn't go to court for $100. Even if you win you lose. Doesn't your time have a value?

Can we sue an attorney for not doing his job properly?

We bought a piece of land and built a house on it. The bank requested a title search and we paid an attorney to have that done. He didn't recommend title insurance - we think he did the search himself. Now, after three years, we find out there's a $20,000 lien against the property by the I.R.S.

■I would sure go after him. That is the advantage of using an attorney - if he makes a mistake, you go after him. He obviously erred with regard to the search. He further erred in not recommending that you have title insurance.

You may have suffered losses because of interest rate changes in the time this has been going on. I would go for liens and expenses. I do not know if it is proper or not in your state, but try to collect what you have lost or will lose in additional interest you have to pay because you could not close escrow at the appropriate time due to his error.

How can I get one dentist to testify against another?

A partial bridge my dentist put on kept loosening. When I went back to him he told me it was due to a jaw disfunction. He tried filing down the partial and putting it back on, but that broke the tooth and now he says he'll have to put in a post. It's causing discomfort and costing a lot of money.

■If you are you thinking about a malpractice suit and you need an expert to testify, there are members of every profession who will do this. Some are actually professional witnesses and they get paid for their testimony. A good malpractice attorney will know professional practitioners who will testify. Assuming there is something to testify about. Frequently patients will say the doctor did this or that, and you examine them and discover that this is not the case.

You will have to prove that all of your problems are a result of negligence on the part of your dentist. I do not know that you can do that. Medicine is not an exact science. First of all you have to find a dentist who agrees, professionally, with what you have told me. This does not sound to me like an area where a malpractice action will be viable. There are not enough dollars involved.

How should I divide assets between my children when I make my will?

I have approximately $100,000. I've always felt it should be equally divided among the four children - that's more democratic, more equitable.

■Why is it necessary to leave the same amount of money to each kid? If one kid needs more and the other needs less, why does it have to be equitable? And since when is there a democracy within the family? If you let your kids vote when they were growing up you must have eaten a lot of peanut butter and ice cream! If you earned the $100,000, why in the world would you ask them who gets it?

I know a lot of parents think this is showing favoritism, but so what? Their needs and desires aren't the same. If one kid needs more and one less, there shouldn't be any problem with that.

You have to do what you feel is necessary with your money, but I don't see any reason for you to try to achieve equality.

How can I keep from declaring personal bankruptcy?

My attorney says I should. I'm 57 years old, my wife took all our joint savings when we seperated and left me with about $6,000 in debts, and I don't have a job right now.

■ I would contact each of the creditors and tell them that you have been advised by counsel to go bankrupt and you do not want to do it. Let them know that you do not have any income. Tell them if they are prepared to put this matter on hold and stop the interest meter, you will make every effort, when your situation changes, to meet your obligations as you would like to do. List every creditor, so everyone knows who is who, and the amounts. Tell them unless all creditors agree, you will be obliged to discharge this obligation through personal bankruptcy which is your last resort.

Unless your attorney thinks you're going to die in the next week or something, what does your age have to do with declaring bankruptcy? You are fifty seven, and you must act like fifty seven. You screwed up. We have all made major mistakes in our lives. You still have a lot of years ahead of you if you are in half way decent health.

I know $6,000 is a great deal of money and you do not have it right now. I've been there. But I am not so certain that this is enough of a debt to justify bankruptcy. A bankruptcy will be with you for the rest of your life.

Who is responsible for putting the wrong size windows in my house addition?

I had an architect draw up the plans, I had a builder come in and do the outside shell for me - including window installation. I was in the process of selling the house when, during final inspection, I found out the windows did not meet the code for fire escape size. I had to pay to get the windows fixed myself since the builder had gone bankrupt.

■Assuming the architect specified the right windows on the plans, then the builder is responsible. But it doesn't really matter. If the builder's business has been legally dissolved according to the rules of your state, you're stuck for it.

What do I have to know to be the executor of my parents' estate?

I was named in their will so do I have to have an attorney? It's not a huge estate. Most of the money is in CDs, a car and a house. How do I divide it up fairly among the six grown children?

■If you are going to do the bulk of the job yourself and you just need an attorney to walk you through it, make that clear to him in the beginning. Just buy an hour of his time.

Laws vary from state to state. Essentially, you will need to open up a trust account with the funds belonging to your mother and father. You will pay all their outstanding bills from that account.

If everything is in equal shares it shouldn't be too tough. I would tell the other heirs that since there is no direction to the will it is your intention to dispose of the house and car as quickly as possible - that you will distribute money and money only.

You will have to go through probate court where you will be given standing by the court so you will be able to dispose of the property - house, CD's, etc.

Regarding other property I would go to your brothers and sisters and say, "Look I will try and work things out - if there is something that belonged to Mom or Dad that you have your eye on, let me know." If more than one of them want the same thing, you may have to make some decisions. They will have to agree that your decision is binding - because legally it is. If they can't agree that your word will be final, tell them you will not consult with any of them and go to it - divide things up the most equitable way you can.

Is there any way I can keep my mother from getting financially hurt in a business deal she loaned me money on?

She loaned me the down payment on a radiator shop. I declared bankruptcy when I got one month and one day behind in payments and the previous owner tacked a notice on the door saying he was repossessing. The tough part is, my mother is on the note as 51% owner, and we owe $7,000 in back taxes.

■I think the damage has been done. There's not much you can do now. The tax obligation is not discharged with bankruptcy unless it is over three years old. So your mom is on the hook for some of those taxes. What you should have done was given your mother a second mortgage on the property. Also, I know you are hard-pressed for money right now but what you should do is have your contract reviewed by an attorney to be certain that the previous owner was allowed to reposses the business the way he did.

Do I have to go through a legal process to get my maiden name back after my divorce?

■You can go through a legal process if you elect to. I don't want to play lawyer, but as I understand it, if you are not out to defraud anybody you can use whatever name you want. If you have title on a home that would change, I would suggest that you have any attorney handle the process. You should change your other documents, bank accounts, etc., yourself. My understanding is that you can go back to using your maiden name without any problems.

Can I represent myself in court on a child support case?

My ex-husband owes me $10,000 and I have a six-year old and a nine-year old to bring up. He doesn't have much money - he only works when he wants to. He had an auto accident about two years ago and he is suing someone. What hurts me the most is that there aren't any assets because he doesn't want there to be. He is working and getting paid under the table.

■You can represent yourself. Start by going to the court and getting copies of evidence in your divorce hearing and documents pertaining to child support. The question is are you wasting your time? If your ex doesn't have money, litigation is not going to help you a whole lot. I do not know if money from a lawsuit can be attached. If he is behind on support payments the court will go after his income tax return - any refund can be attached. As to his working and getting money under the table - knowing that and proving it are two different things.

Can I collect $210 for interruption of orthodontic treatment?

Our son was assaulted at school by another student. The only thing that kept his front teeth from going down his throat were his braces. I'm getting ready to go to small claims court. Unfortunately, the other boy is from another country and is living here with a guardian. We don't have parents or a household to slap a lien against. Our medical expenses total $74 from the emergency clinic and $145 from the orthodontist.

■I doubt if you can tack on the additional expense, and frankly I don't believe you are going to collect anything. If you want to cause the guardians of this kid some problems, okay. But you'll have an empty victory. If you win, who is going to pay you? If it were me, I would teach my kid to fight.

CHAPTER 6 *Credit*

" Rather than worry about your credit, worry about getting the bills paid - then rebuild your credit. "

When you're late with payments, how long do credit card companies go before they actually start taking legal action?

I'm not able to make the payments on my credit cards. I owe about $8,000. I'm 27, married with two kids. Our income has dropped to $600 per month. My wife has tried working to bring in additional income, but we have young kids and it doesn't work.

■You have two choices in circumstances of this kind. One would be to decrease outgo or increase income. When you have decreased the outgo as much as you can, you try to increase income. If your wife can't leave the kids during the day, she could get a night job. That will cut down in your social life, but it's a way to dig out from under this.

If you feel that you cannot manage, then you want to sit down with a non-profit credit counselor. They are in a far better position to negotiate with the credit vendors than you are. They have some standing, where you do not. What the counselor will do is negotiate a payment schedule that you can live with. You only get one bite at the apple. If you agree to pay an amount, stick to it.

You are in deep trouble. You are talking about being in hock for a full year's income, with 20% interest tacked on to that. You've made some mistakes, it's time to go out and pay for them. I don't know of any other recourse. Don't even think about bankruptcy. That would be absurd for the small amount of money you owe. It would take years to get past the effects of that.

Should I borrow money from a line of credit at a lower interest rate to pay off credit card purchases?

If I had a $1500 line of credit on my credit card, and I charged purchases of $500, then I have $1000 left on the line of credit. Wouldn't I save money if I borrowed against the line of credit, at a lower rate, and used it to pay off the $500?

■Certainly. If your company offers a lower interest rate on the cash advance you can borrow cash against your credit card for less than you have to pay on purchases. The difference in interest charges usually ranges between 6% and 7% from low to high.

We are talking about many credit cards, not all, and we are talking about the bank cards. If you have a credit line, you can borrow money on your credit card. They'll even send you checks in the mail. More often than not, the interest rate on those loans is lower than you would pay on the unpaid balance on your credit card as a result of purchases. So what you can do is borrow money from the same people, pay off your installment loans, and save a bit of money. I learn something new from you folks everyday. But I strongly urge you to check with your credit card company to see if your idea really works this way.

How can I avoid legal action while I pull myself out of debt?

A couple of my creditors have threatened legal action and repossession. I'm about thirty to sixty days behind on my cars. I would love to get rid of them, but I think they're worth less than what I still owe on them. In four or five months I could pull myself out. My wife and I are now making about $46,000 and our debts are about $23,000, including the cars which are worth about $10,000 if I sold them. I'm wondering how my credit is going to survive this. Is bankruptcy an alternative?

■I think that you have let things go. You need to use a non-profit credit counselor to help mediate for you. But, the closer you get to repossession the more difficult you make it for them to negotiate. I think that would probably be your best option. Call a Social Service office in your area for a name. What they will do is try to negotiate with your creditors. You will make payments to them and they will apportion the money out every month. The creditor will pay for their services

You're between a rock and a hard place with those cars. You are well aware your equity in the cars is not sufficient to retire your obligations and you cannot sell them unless you pay them off. If they repossess them, you will be responsible for the difference between what the finance company sells the cars for and what you owe. That figure could be substantially greater yet. You'll need to rely on the credit counselors working something out with the lenders.

But, lets look at your total debt situation. You are only in for under $10,000 actually. You should not have too much trouble bailing out. Right now, rather than worry about your credit, worry about getting the bills paid. Then rebuild your credit after the fact. You have already been in default and you are in default now. Your credit is pretty badly bruised. But, if you built it up once, there is no reason why you can't do it again.

A bankruptcy is out of the question. The last thing you need in your background at your age is bankruptcy for less than $10,000.

Is making payments by automatic deduction a good idea?

That's the way I'm currently making my health spa membership payments. Isn't that similar to power of attorney? What if he goes belly up and sells the spa? In a situation like that, what would keep them from continuing to deduct the money?

■I would not want to get involved in a situation like that. I realize that the reason the merchant likes it is because it makes life a little easier on him - less paperwork and probably fewer late payments. That's all very nice, but it also means he gets all the float and you get nothing.

It is not power of attorney because it can't be withdrawn at anytime. As far as the stability of the company and whether they're going out of business - I do not understand how you could get burned. Let's assume that the first of month is rolling around. If you know the place went belly up, you would be down at the bank that morning putting a stop on the automatic withdrawal permission. What are you worried about in that respect? Stop loosing sleep over it.

Can my credit be damaged by a loan company?

The company has been notifying me that my loan payments are late, when they're not. There have been no late charges, but I don't want this to damage my credit rating. I'm making a $50 student loan payment to an agency out of state. For some reason, it's taking them a long time to process it. The check is stamped paid on the back about a month after I send it. There have been no late charges, but I don't want this to damage my credit rating.

■Why don't you send it certified mail and see what happens? That would just give you an idea of when they are actually receiving it. I don't know of any agency that would be concerned with this right now. You have not been damaged. One way to kill the problem is spend an extra $50. You would not lose the $50.00, just pay them one month in advance. I'm not telling you that this is right, but if you just want to remedy the problem pragmatically, send them two payments next time. You would only lose the interest on $50 which is not exactly a huge amount of money.

They are wrong. But you have an immediate remedy. I'll grant you, it's probably not very satisfying, but it fixes the problem.

Should I pay a bill I don't owe to protect my credit?

I closed my business down in 1985. A year and two months after I closed the business, I got this letter from a collection agency that I had not paid my workers comp for this year. I explained that my business hasn't been in operation for two years, but I'm still getting notices and they won't even talk to me about it. I'm worried about my credit.

■I wouldn't pay it in a million years. I would notify the collection agency and the insurance agency in writing that you are putting this matter in dispute, that your enterprise was not operative in 1987 and that you attempted to call and they refused to talk to you any further, but you wish to notify them that if any damage accrues to your credit reputation because of their error, you will hold them civilly responsible.

Can a new management company make changes in an installment contract?

My racquetball club went bankrupt and my payment contract was picked up by a new management company who told me there were new contract restrictions.

■They can't make any changes whatever. The contract may or may not have been assignable. But they have absolutely no right, unless you gave it to them on the contract - to change the rules in the middle of the game. You want things to go on exactly as before. And since they chose to change the rules, you are probably free to make other arrangements. But there is no question in my mind that when a contract is assigned it can't be changed without the agreement of both parties.

Can a finance company do anything they want to to collect on a debt?

I purchased a used vehicle a few months back. Right after that the small business I own ran into a lot of problems. I sent the finance company a letter stating I would not be able to make the first payment, but I would try to catch up as soon as possible. Afterward, instead of sending me a letter or anything, they started contacting my neighbors and places I do business with. They wanted details about a lot of personal things - how much I owe, what I had financed and that sort of thing.

■No, they cannot do anything they want to collect the debt. They cannot call you in the middle of the night, they cannot harrass you, but to inquire as to what your financial position is by calling the people you do business with, I would guess they can do that. It may be embarassing for you and it may jeopardize your credit standing, but I think they can do it.

I think what the finance company is looking at is the possibility of fraud. I think they are trying to find out if you have snowed them or not. It might be a little different if you had a 36 month note and you paid off 25 months, but here you went out and borrowed the money and have not paid back a penny. They get nervous about those things.

I don't know why you expect a letter in reply from them. What's to reply? You did not pay them. You are in default on your car. What more is there to say?

Should my doctor have turned my bill over to a collection agency and ruined my credit?

I needed a set of X-rays and I went to the X-ray department and asked them how much the total procedure would cost? Hospital charges, radiology charges, doctor fees, etc. They said $75 and I said fantastic, I'll have the procedure done. I was unemployed at the time and was concerned about money. A month later I received two bills, one for $125 and one for $75.

■I'll bet $75 was for the hospital and $125 was for the radiologist. Usually there's a sign that says the cost for the X-rays is separate from the radiologist fees. But, since you specifically asked for all expenses, perhaps you should write a letter to be included in your file at the credit reporting company. Explain exactly what happened. How, even when you specifically asked about fees, you were misled. You can also say in the letter that you intend to pay the bill in installments that you are capable of handling. Beyond that there isn't a whole lot you can do.

CHAPTER 7 *Business*

" Ideas are worth about 2 1/2 cents apiece in bulk. If that. "

How do you start a newsletter?

I have an idea to develop an educational newsletter for young investors. At this point I have the materials and the ideas together, but I don't know where to go to find someone who can tell me about test marketing and response rates and what to do from this point on. The real problem is that to do the test marketing with a direct mail campaign would cost several thousand dollars.

■Would you believe there is a newsletter that is written for people who write newsletters? I think you ought to take a look at that to begin with. There are also seminars held for people who want to start newsletters. Just talk to the people who are in the business and you can learn.

You will have to register with the Securities and Exchange Commission. I do not see how you can do what you described without giving investment advice. I certainly would want you to get another opinion on that. Find out if you are going to be violating the Security and Exchange Commission's laws. Beyond that, how do you plan on reaching people to inform them that the newsletter exists?

If you use direct mail, you have to have a list of names and addresses. You have to establish a criteria by which to select the list. You are going to have to spend some money to get your test marketing accomplished. If you are not willing to do that then you do not want it very bad. I do not mean that unkindly. Several thousand dollars is nothing.

I saw some stuff go out of our office today that was 3,000 to 5,000 pieces just to explore an idea with some of the people we mail to. It costs about $1.00 apiece for that one little sampling. These things just do not happen without money. If you think you have a good idea, you have to spend $5,000 to $20,000, and that is not a whole lot of money, to test it out. That is what it takes. You cannot do it for a whole lot less. Unfortunately, those are the facts.

We all have great ideas until it comes time to write the check and then reality strikes. I cannot imagine even running a test on something like this without spending close to $10,000.

No one can be sure what to expect for a response rate. Let me give you some examples of that. One item I tested got a 13% response rate, which is incredible. Thirteen out of 100 responded. On another we got 3/10 of 1% or 3 on 1,000. It depends on what you are selling and how much you are selling it for. If you're looking at 3 in 1,000, you better have a very profitable enterprise.

On the three in 1,000, we only sold one in three. That meant we had to put 1,000 pieces of literature out to sell 1 item. You are not going to have that with $30 newsletters, are you? So on the other side of that, if you were selling $300 newsletters to 13% of your mailing, you could hit it big.

You have got to figure out what response rate you need to stay in business. If you can't get it, then you are out of business and you have to go out and do something else. When you test, you can't try it with 100 pieces either. You have to do it with several thousand. You know that you can make a mistake if you pick the wrong list. Or if you make a supposition on a wrong list, that can kill you too. If the particular list you used did better than your full market run will do, you have a problem. Oh boy, I have 10% response on the test, only to find that you had a super test list and that the regular list doesn't do that well. There are a lot of pitfalls.

To go after millions requires some dough and risks. You have to make the decision whether or not you want to risk your bankroll, so that you could be the beneficiary.

What's the best way to start up a secretarial service business?

I have years of experience as a secretary and I'd like something that would give me a little more control over my future.

■First, you've got to consider how you would go about reaching your prospective customers. Probably the only way you can find out if there is a need for any service is to promote that service. Put the hook in the water, bait it and see if somebody nibbles.

Probably the best approach, initially, would be solicitation. Personal solicitation - walk in cold or by phone. Any other advertising etc. is too expensive for you. I happen to believe in radio, but I'm not sure I would recommend it to you because you are only advertising you - one person. And the cost could not be spread across a big enough base.

If your family can get along without your paycheck for awhile, then solicitation would make a lot of sense. It may be a little slower, but it is not costly, except in terms of your body. You've gotta get out there and slug it out.

Next, you have to establish your fees. The answer to that is to find out what the traffic will bear. Determine what your competition is charging by soliciting them. You can do that now, while you are working. For example, one of your competitors will be the temporary services, right? Find out what it costs to place a temporary. You should know that anyway if you work in an office.

Try to make yourself a tad different. Are you willing to work all night on a rush job? Frequently there's that kind of instant demand for extraordinary service. If you can offer that kind of help you may have something going for you. You could include meeting planning, travel planning, business group functions, that sort of thing.

Correlate your thoughts, put them in order, and put a little brochure together. You are going to be dealing with small companies, because the big companies are going to have somebody doing these functions. The brochure could say something like..."If your company doesn't have a travel planner, you ought to be talking to Mary Jane, let Mary Jane do it for you", and so forth. See if anybody will nibble.

Sample the market. Unfortunately there is no shortcut to that. You and I could have a great idea but we don't know if it is going to live in the marketplace until we put it out there. I wish you well.

Do I market a candy product myself or hand it over to a chocolate company?

I have an idea for a new chocolate candy, a new shape. I tried it at Christmas on a few friends and they loved it. They said it was so simple why hadn't anybody else done it before? I have a great name and a catchy phrase and it all fits together perfectly. I am designing my packaging now and I have some relatives who own a printing company so they can help me package it.

■Ideas are worth about 2 1/2 cents apiece in bulk. If that. You have to have the ability to manufacture and the ability to advertise for your idea to be worth something. And it has to be something unique that people can't find anywhere else, or at least not around the corner. That's the really hard part.

Everybody is looking for a pet rock. I have to assume we are talking about a local product, at least at first. I mean you are not going to Hershey. It is just not going to happen. I don't believe that they will talk to you.

Now, unless you want to go into the chocolate business yourself, I have to believe that somewhere in your area there is a chocolatier that already has the equipment to mold and manufacture chocolate. Consider trying to interest them in a joint venture, where you have the idea and you license them to produce it. But first take some steps to protect yourself.

Unfortunately, you can't protect the idea. A manufacturer could duplicate it as soon as you hit the market with it. But you can at least protect the name. Form a corporation and at least protect the name in your state.

When you cut your deal with the chocolatier, try to get a piece of the local market. If the idea is really unique, really super unique, you may be able to sell some by mail order.

Regards packaging - it is one thing to own a printing company and another to package. You have to have a way to get the candy into the boxes, unless you do it by hand and then you have to be able to do it in a sanitary fashion because it is an edible product, which is a lot different from packaging a pet rock.

How do I price and market a houseware product?

My wife and I have a patent pending on a houseware product. It's going to cost about $1.50 each, which includes packaging, everything, ready to go. We think it should retail for under ten dollars. And, to lessen our up front risk, can we sell it with a six month delivery time?

■If it costs you $1.50 and that's everything in, you've got to sell it for about $3.00, the distributors have to sell it for $4.50 and the retailer for $8.95. That's pretty loose, but it's about right.

As to marketing it, you are going to have to deal with distributors, you won't be able to sell directly to retailers. You don't have the credit capability, you don't have the shipping capability, plus you're only selling one item. The distributor is selling towel racks, paper holders, medicine cabinets, a dozen items, right? He can afford to have a guy calling on retailers. When you're selling just one item, you can't.

If you ask most distributors to order from you then ask them to wait for six months for delivery - unless it's a Christmas product - they'll laugh at you. Ordinarily they want the stuff in three weeks, a month, or less. If it were my product, I would rather have it ready to ship. But that requires two things: some gambling and some investment. I am a risk taker. If I believe in what I'm doing, then I'm willing to go the whole nine yards. Maybe I'm wrong, maybe I'm heading for a brick wall, but I think you're going to find an ocean of people who will tell you to take a hike.

Say you persuaded me the stuff belongs in my store, now persuade me to wait six months. How do you do that? Maybe you could talk a few department stores into it, but you can't do business just with department stores. You are going to need the independents. I guarantee that the distributors are not going to work six months in advance with you. If you tell a commission salesman he's not getting paid for six months, just for your convenience, is he going to push your product very hard?

So many people never want to paint themselves into a corner. It seems to me that the way to be successful is get in a corner and fight your way out. That's just one man's opinion.

What is the most equitable way for my son to establish charges for his gardening services?

I am trying to get my 13 year old son involved in a little garden- ing enterprise this summer. Should he charge by the hour, square yard, or job?

■Charge by the job. Here's why. I do not know how long it is going to take my gardener to cut the grass. But, I don't care because I pay him by the month. If you come up to me and say you are going to charge me so many hours, I would want to know how many hours it would take to cut it. Why complicate it. Just say it will cost $10 to get your grass cut or whatever the amount.

But before you send him out there with his lawnmower and little receipt book, there's a bigger problem. I don't want to rain on your parade, but...anybody who lets a 13 year old cut their grass is looking for big trouble. There are all kinds of laws against kids using power equipment for hire. Your neighbors are in some jeopardy if they hire him. Your area probably has specific laws which prohibit him from working and using power equipment - for obvious reasons. People can lose fingers, arms and feet in those things.

As far as your own liability is concerned as a parent, I do not think they can lay it on you for child abuse. I doubt it seriously. Nothing is going to happen until there is an injury. Then there is a problem.

Should I pay a salary to my partner before he actually relocates and starts working for the company?

I offered my brother a 49% partnership in my company. I need a good salesman and he's it. He sent me half of the purchase price. The trouble is he can't relocate and come to work until he sells his house, but he wants a salary now.

■I'd tell him, "Look brother, you have ten days to get here or the deal's off, and I'll send your money back."

Frequently, folks have to leave where they are and go some place else to make their living. Now, unless his wife is incompetent, there is no reason why she can't handle the sale of the house, button up the kids, the packing, whatever, and then move on down after him. He can probably move in with you for the time being.

I would give him that option. If he is not dedicated to what you want to do - he may be your brother, and you may love him - you wouldn't want him as a partner.

What should be my concerns in starting up a children's apparel business?

It involves importing certain infant's and children's knitted apparel from a foreign country. I plan to sell to small specialty shops in the area and advertise in local newspapers.

■First, do you have product liability insurance? You ought to have some. What happens if some kid gets a doll? The kid chews on it and gets sick. Or burns to death. A million things. Just about anything that you produce requires product liability insurance. The cost of insurance depends upon what the insurer sees as your exposure. If you have, for example, a food item...that's going to cost a little bit more because it's ingested. But some things that might be ingested accidentally, can cost more. So that's the first thing you have to start with.

Next, do you have any kind of an agreement that protects your rights with the manufacturer or importer, in case the business catches on? Let's assume that you go out and build up a market. You want exclusivity for a fairly good size territory - certainly east of the Mississippi; or the responsibility to meet certain sales figures over a period of time. What's to prevent them from jerking the string on you anytime? Cutting off your supply. If they go out of business, decide they don't want to do business with you or who knows what, where are you? It is very difficult when anybody is captive. And captive in this sense means a one source of supply operation. You are at their mercy. Something to be considered, that's all.

How can I persuade a partner to buy my share of the business?

Some time back, one of my partners put pressure on me to get out of the partnership. But now that it's in financial trouble and I'd like to sell, he's not acting. I could use the money because I put my house up for collateral to finance the business and the bank is after me.

■Probably the only thing you may be able to do is find somebody else to buy you out. You would be better off finding a third party that would buy you out at a discount. If your partner balks, it's probably because the best thing in the world he could do is stall. He is trying to sweat you out. I can understand that, but I would not let him get away with it. That says a lot about partnerships.

How do I go about negotiating a price for my gardening services?

I have been in gardening for thirty years. I make $8.57 an hour now. I interviewed for a job at a new $300,000 home and the guy wants to pay minimum wage.

■He will if he can get away with it. I would look elsewhere. I'm paying a guy a whole lot more than minimum wage to do my place. If you're talking about doing seasonal work on a full time basis, I would stress why you're worth more. You are more efficient. Don't do it by the hour, do it by the job. Charge so much for each job.

How do you market a new artist?

How do you find a source for financing? What about getting into galleries or department stores?

■Go to the shows in Los Angeles, San Francisco, Dallas, New York - the major art shows. An artist may fall more in the gift segment rather than serious art. You may want to go to a gift show and get a feel for who is handling various types of sculpture or whatever - and take some samples along. The first step is to produce and prove that the public will buy.

The chances are that the buyer is not going to say hello to an unknown artist. Buyers work from an approved list. Unless an artist is on it, they cannot buy, even if they do like his work.

As far as the financing is concerned, finding someone who is willing to invest is a whole different story. Although there are many galleries that will take a chance at an unknown, until such time as he establishes a name for himself, he is going to have to come up with it out of his own pocket - a little bit of money to produce, at least on a limited basis, and then start getting out and hitting the bricks.

What do I need to know about buying a franchise?

The company wants to establish some dealerships now, and then later start to franchise. They are trying to push me to make a decision. Normally they want $60,000 for an exclusive dealership. But, because of my experience as an engineer, they are offering it to me exclusively for just $7,500.

■This is a new company. They don't have a name. What are they going to do for you that you cannot do for yourself?Advertising? You can do that for yourself. If there's training, consider how much it would cost you for the same thing.

Let's examine the price. They attached a value of $60,000. Now they're going to sell it to you for 1/8 of the actual value. That makes them look like Santa Claus. That should make you nervous. I say nonsense. You may decide you need them, but you should certainly explore the possibility of doing it yourself.

There are very good and sufficient reasons to buy dealerships and franchises and otherwise associate yourself with other companies, but you've got to evaluate them carefully.

Will a bank lend me money to start a business?

I am 23 years old and I am looking to buy a dry cleaning business. I have gone to a couple of business brokers and some businesses are selling for $80,000 to $130,000, depending on the location. A lot of the businesses that I have talked to want 30% down and they will finance the rest.

■There is no way in the world, at the age of 23, that you are going to be able to borrow the down payment on a business from a bank. It is not going to happen. The bank is not in the business of loaning venture capital for two reasons. One, it is a small deal, and two, they want your life. It is understandable that they want your life. I think your best bet would be to look for a widow or an estate or someone who does not want their business and is having a tough time selling it.

Where would you look for someone like that? Advertise. Put an ad in the paper for somebody who just wants out badly enough. I mean they have had it. I have sold a business to a young guy and financed the whole thing. I did that because I had a better shot at getting all my money from him rather than getting a down payment from someone else and not seeing the rest of the money.

You have to persuade someone that you are the best thing since sliced bread. You are willing to work twenty five hours a day and you know something about the business. Tell them that you will work for them as a salaried employee at a relatively low salary for a year, if they will put in writing the fact that they will carry all the paper for you a year from now, if you prove yourself.

It is important that they know you are honest and you are not going to beat them out of any money and you will pay the premium price if they carry all of the paper. You are not going to find one of those in two minutes time. But, those kinds of deals are around. What you're selling is you. You have to impress them that you are beyond reproach, you have integrity - the whole nine yards.

I know it can be done because I have done it. There are a lot of ways. I have been the guy who has done the financing and the guy who got financed.

How can I increase revenue operating a van-pooling service?

I lease a van and I am finding that, after collecting my rider fees, I have to come up with more money to pay for my lease, gas and maintenance. The problem is that I dropped two riders. Also I am trying to find out if there is a possibility of getting corporate sponsorship for the van itself. What if I contacted the local Automobile Dealers Association about sponsorship? Maybe they could advertise on the van.

■I think your primary problem, as I see it, is that you are probably priced too low. You are making the error that many landlords make. You figure on 100% occupancy, which does not work all the time. Figure two seats will be empty. If there are twelve seats in the van, take one out for the driver and divide your costs by nine, not eleven.

Secondly, you may not be able to use a private van for what you are talking about. I don't know, but in a lot of places the various car pooling regulations shut private guys down - they say you are competition with licensed bus operators.

I have a couple of problems with finding commercial sponsors. One is you may not be able to put a sign on the side of a private van in your area. Secondly, is this sponsor willing to foot the bill for the van just for running his name on the side of it?

Now, as far as corporate sponsorship is concerned, you might approach an employer with the idea. Perhaps by using you they could provide free transportation service to get better employees. It would help keep their parking lot free for customers and assure that their employees get there on time.

You may find a whole boat load from one place. That is what I would be looking for. You may be able to find a company that is willing to underwrite it to some extent.

How do I publish and distribute a book privately?

I do not want to sell the rights to anything I write. I want to control them.

■The clear answer is you hire a printer or one of the "vanity press" houses to print your book. Then you go out and sell it.

The conventional method is that you submit it to a publisher. If they're interested in publishing, you sign an agreement that says they publish and market the book and you get a royalty. The contract spells out how long they have the rights to publish. After that, it's yours again.

If you're lucky, the publisher pays you an advance. It could be a huge amount of money, it could be a modest amount of money, or it could be none. Usually it is a symbolic amount.

When you're looking at the cost of publishing your own book, the question is, how far is up? You can have 200 copies run off for under $4000 or $5000. Maybe $2,000 will get you some copies. But then how do you get them to market? In all likelihood bookstores are not going to even say hello to you.

The publisher absorbs the expense of proofing, printing, binding, etc. Then they distribute it to the stores. There is nothing to prevent you from doing all these things yourself as long as you have very, very deep pockets. But, can you do them as well as the publisher? That's his craft. He doesn't write. You don't publish.

How can we get additional parking for our business?

My husband and I own a general rental store. We're out of storage room and we need more parking. Our building is currently 3200 square feet and we own the adjacent lot, but we'll need that for our additional storage structure.

■First thing you will do is a square foot analysis on the present building. You need to know exactly how many dollars each square foot is bringing in. What's making you money and what isn't. You want to know how many dollars, in volume, per square foot. If you divide that 3200 into the total number of dollars generated per year, that's what your square foot volume is, right? There may be merchandise or equipment you may want to get rid of. A lot of the stuff you rent is only rented for a portion of the year, isn't that true? You don't turn it over often enough. It's eating up space. That is the first thing I would look at.

The next thing I would do is improve your parking. I'm telling you one thing, if I come down there for a post hole digger and see the lot full, I go somewhere else. If you don't have parking - I don't care what you carry - in today's society, nobody patronizes you. Use the land for parking and go to a second story for building expansion.

Put a piston elevator in. You can put your heavy stuff on the primary work floor. Put your lighter stuff...lawn mowers and the seasonal stuff on the second floor.

Should I invest in a new truck now or wait till business demands it?

I own a courier service and I just won a lawsuit for $15,000. So I can afford to buy a larger truck.

■Why would you go out and buy it before you need it? Let's assume that you did not have the lawsuit, what would you have done?

Keep that money as a cushion for the business. If your business is growing in a decent fashion, why change the direction of your enterprise because of the windfall?

I would put that money in some kind of money fund or whatever, where it is liquid. Keep it there for emergencies. A business without a cushion is always on the razor's edge. I'd rather have that cushion.

What would be a fair rate for the TV station to charge me on a "PS" (Per Sale) or "PI" (Per Inquiry) basis?

I have found a product I would like to sell on TV on a "per Inquiry" basis. I will sell two of them for $19.95 plus $4.00 shipping and handling. Also, should I have some kind of an insurance? It's a mechanical bird that flaps it's wings.

■They are going to want something like between 40 and 50% of the purchase price for a PI deal. But, before we get too far along, there's a big difference between "PI" and "PS." "PI", or per inquiry, means you pay even if a caller just asks for information...whether you sold it or not. "PS" means per sale You are looking for a "PS" deal. That's not including your $4.00 for handling. The shipping and handling is a way to grab a little extra money and keep the price down, theoretically.

In regard to insurance: absolutely. Any product that you have your imprint on must be insured. If one of these things flaps its wings and flies into some child, putting his eye out, you will hear about it.

Can I bring legal action against my father's partners to change their requirements in regard to selling the business?

The corporation's bylaws say that if a shareholder dies, the remaining 3 partners have to buy out his heirs at a fixed share value, even though those values have increased substantially over the years. My father wants to change the stipulation, they do not. Their argument is that they do not have the cash if something would happen.

■You can always bring an action against somebody, but it's costly and the question then is...is it worth it? If you did, you would consult an attorney and he would look for a precedent - a similar case. That is what you pay the attorney for. If there is such a case, he will build his case on that. They say there is no such thing as law until there has been a precedent. I cannot believe that you are plowing new turf. But it will cost a ton of money in court.

Here's what I would do: get to the root of the problem. I would sit down and talk with these people. I would want to know why they won't consider changing the arrangement. It is kind of stupid to play last man club, because that's what you are doing. The last guy left alive is the beneficiary.

Is there a tax consideration? The IRS will not stand still for this if there are tax consequences. Get an opinion from an accountant who knows IRS laws.

Tell them that you will go to court. Suggest that the assets be appraised and each will choose an appraiser. Try to compromise.

Now the guys say that they cannot raise the money. You have to have an answer for that. One of the answers is that we can appreciate that, but we will have a three year buy-out period where assets can be liquidated to raise the money, but we would still establish a real estate price. That is one possible answer.

How do we set the price on a business we're trying to sell?

My husband is trying to sell his interest in a two-way radio repair shop. He owns a third of it. The owner won't help us find a buyer. It's only making $50,000 per year. We're trying to sell it for $120,000.

■That is too much money, in my opinion. What your husband has right now is a medium priced job. If you had $120,000 to invest some place and if you invested it in bonds, you could probably look for about a 10% return. That's $12,000 a year. It is really only bringing in $38,000, because the capital - the $120,000 - is worth something. Your shop is just not bringing in the kind of income to defend that price. Sale is basically a function of price. You will have to increase the terms and you don't have a whole lot of control over that because of your partner.

Think about this. Tell the salesmen who call on you, who have their finger on the pulse of the market, that you will throw them $5,000 if they bring you a buyer.

Is it smart to operate a business from a distance?

I would like to open up a shop on a mall. The only problem is, I would have to commute about 800 miles. My wife thinks I'm insane.

■If you know the business - the traffic, what you can afford to pay per square foot, and how much volume you have to do to pay the rent and the help - it may not be so insane. The question is...how many trips do you have to make? That is a practical matter. Look for a manager who can use a PC (computer). Advertise for help, but make it clear that the person gets paid on performance. You could even make the manager a minor league partner with some responsibility.

The difficulty you may or may not have also depends on the complexity of the business. Your business has one major thing going for it - you operate an enterprise which is controllable by inventory. Your manager can control the inventories by computer and, through a telephone modem, you can dial up the computer and know exactly where you are on a day-to-day basis. There are a great many things you can do from long range in the kind of business you are considering.

Whether that mall is two miles from where you are or 2,000, a business analysis and game plan has to stand on its own. If it does, and you really see an opportunity there - given the things I described - I do not see why you shouldn't investigate it further.

How do we determine which radio station in our market is the best one to advertise on?

We have talked to three or four stations in town and every one of them tell us that they are the best one for us.

■When you consider any advertising vehicle, you have to consider what you are selling and who you are trying to sell it to. If you advertise rock tickets for the next concerts of the Grateful Dead, the stations that carry my show are not the place to put the commercials. That is a fact. On the other side of that, if you are advertising a middle to up-scale product where you want someone to spend a couple pennies, the acid-rock station is not the place to be. Each station has a different clientele.

You are far more apt to have people who own their own business listening to a program like mine, than you are to a heavy rock station, are you not?

Take a look at the people who are buying your product. Create a profile of that customer. You want to find a station that reaches the demographics (age, sex, where they live, when they listen) which are as close to that profile as you can get. You have to see who the station is reaching.

How much can I charge for a consulting fee?

I figure I will be able to bring a company $3 million in new business in a year, based on my capital expenditure recommendations. I was thinking of a fee of around $7,500.

■In establishing a value to a client, you need to find out how many others can provide the same service. If your client cannot go out and do this on his own - with a reasonable expectation of success, without the trial and error that could cost him a lot more dough than your fee - I think you are on solid ground.

If you can prove that you can return the kind of money you're talking about, I do not think $100,000 would be an unreasonable fee. If you are a good salesman and can show them on paper that you are going to get their capital back and increase their revenue to show that kind of profit, after your fee, I think they would be interested.

You should ask for some money up front plus a contract that your attorney approves. You can bet your life that their attorney will approve any contract they enter into. You owe yourself the same protection.

How do I get out of a small video rental business?

Recently a lot of competition has come in - big national companies - able to rent at ridiculously low prices. I can't compete. I'm not making any money. I tried to sell my inventory to the competition, but they're not interested.

■The thing is, when you get into an enterprise that is not making it, you have to cut your losses. That is a very difficult thing to do. The first time is the worst time. It will not be worth more money today than it was yesterday. Sit down and figure out how you can liquidate it in the best possible way.

One way may be to have a sale to the public. There are people who buy video tapes. You may have a table at a flea market. It costs very little. What do you lose? Mark the tapes at a price that you can afford to settle for. Have a retail sale. Advertise in the newspaper - "videos for sale." You may have to do it in stages, but you will get some of your money back.

How can I raise $200,000 to start up a day care center?

I am thinking of forming a limited partnership and approaching people to invest $10,000 each. I have a lot of experience in the child-care area - in terms of setting the business up, looking for the site and hiring - and that would be my part of the investment.

■Limited partnerships are certainly a viable way to put packages together, but if you come to me, please do not tell me about your expertise. I am very skeptical. If you are so good, why don't you have any money? I want to know how much are you putting into this deal? If you say you are going to put your expertise in, I will show you the door. You have nothing at risk but a little bit of your time. What are you risking? Nothing. I want to know that you have something on the line.

I hope that it works out for you, but you better have something more to come to the store with than you are walking in with right now. All you have is an idea and ideas are 2 1/2 cents apiece. Or less.

Does a "non-profit" status exist where some profit is allowed?

A New York theater wants to do a production of my play. I have to raise half of the money for the production - about $11,000. We would split the box office receipts unless the production is a great success, in which case we would form a limited partnership. The theater has a special non-profit status which would effect the profitability of the production.

■I would have the non-profit status thoroughly approved by an attorney, one that is conversant with tax laws, because you could get yourself in a world of trouble trying to mix non-profit and profit. Non-profit organizations have obligations in terms of getting rid of their money, etc. You should take a look at a non-profit charter before you arrange go ahead with this. Also a contract must address what you mean by a "great success," since you have established that as the criteria in forming a limited partnership.

Am I spending my advertising money wisely in The Yellow Pages?

I am contemplating spending $600 a month on a half-page ad in the yellow pages for my truck and trailer rental business.

■I think you picked the vehicle of first choice, if I were in your position. When you think about renting something, where is the first place you go, if you don't know anyone? I would want to be advertising in the market that I was trying to penetrate.

There is also something to be said for supplemental advertising, because there is another part of this equation. If there are two ads on a page - one I recognize and the other I've never heard of - I am more apt to call the name that I recognize. I would supplement the yellow pages, if I could. But, if I had only one place to go, I would be in the yellow pages.

How much good faith money should I ask from a firm that is going to manufacture and market my design?

I designed and built the mold for a plastic railroad tie. The manufacturer will pay me a royalty on every unit sold. I've put about $15,000 into it. I figure the mold itself is worth $6,000.

■There is no magic formula. The amount can be whatever you both agree on. What are your options? Suppose the guy says this is the deal and if you do not like it, good-bye. You would have to find someone else to market it for you. How difficult would that be? You still have to make a decision in your own mind. I want to know if he has a gun to your head or are you holding the gun. Maybe it's somewhere in between. You are going to have to decide that before you know how much hard ball you can play.

Also you need an escape clause. If he doesn't move x-number of units in a mutually agreed upon time, then the deal is off. I would give it a year.

You retain ownership of the mold. I do not think that should be a negotiable point. It's my opinion that the mold should remain your property and I would have it so stated in any agreement.

Should I go into partnership with my current employer?

She owns a day-care business - a small school with the capacity for 80 children. We would like to open another school in the area. The problem is that her present center is $177,000 in debt and it's going to take about fifteen years to pay it off. The reason I am considering this woman as a partner is that her school is respected and she has four years experience. Also, I would like the moral support. I'm a little scared to go it on my own.

■I was in the day care business for fourteen years. We started with nine kids and wound up with 400.

First, if you are too scared without someone propping you up, then I think you ought to be an employee some place. If you had said to me that she had all the academic credentials and you cannot get into business without those, then that could be a good reason to have her as a partner. Although it is also true that you can hire people with academic credentials.

This woman is obviously not capitalized, otherwise she would not be in debt up to her eyeballs. She is not bringing a whole lot of money into this marriage. What is she bringing? She may be a lovely lady, but I would not do it.

It may be that the neighborhood is ready for another day care center. In my opinion, though, there is no reason in the world you should get tied up with a lady who herself has a real alligator on her hands. I do not think it would be a good marriage.

How do my partner and I split up without having either one of us legally responsible for the other's actions?

We want to function separately, doing the same business in different areas. I own half the stock in the corporation, he owns the other half.

■Ordinarily when you have a small corporation and you have a change of ownership, you dissolve the corporation. You guys are partners right now and you are both responsible. Let's assume you did some work six months ago and all of a sudden three months from now they have a real problem. Now he is history because you bought him out, and the people with the problem will come after the corporation, which is now all yours. The fact that the stock ownership has changed does not relieve the corporation of any responsibility. You are now on the hook for the whole thing.

If I were buying a small business, say it is the XYZ Company, I would dissolve it and call it the XXX Company. Or, I would use the name as a trade style, but have a new corporation as the parent. That way you are not responsible for any previous. If you are absolutely clean and you want to take a chance, be my guest. All you do is have his stock transferred to you which takes him off. Have a corporate meeting and have him formally resign.

How can I relieve myself of any responsibility for my former partner's activities?

Our business operated in three cities. He wants to operate in two and I would like the other one.

■One way would be to license him under your current corporation, but you may have some responsibility under the license. The issue of responsibility depends on a lot of things. First of all the contractual relationship between your corporation as a parent and his corporation as a licensee. The license can be part of the compensation when he takes off.

The most obvious way is to form a separate corporation. You could form the Jones Company of Dayton and then the Jones Company of Cincinnati with the agreement of the guy who has the older company. The one you must be concerned about is the corporation that you are going to continue with.

But, all of these things have to be done under the guidance of a competent attorney.

How can I market one of my mother's old family recipes?

It's a topping recipe to use with dessert. How can I protect my idea? Can I test the product with friends and folks at work and church?

■First, you cannot copyright a flavor. All you can protect is the name of the flavor.

As far as the testing is concerned...as long as you are doing that on a friendly basis, I guess you are okay. As soon as you get a little broader, you have a product liability problem. If someone were to break out in a rash or alleged that their toenails fell off because they ate this stuff, you would have a problem.

Let's assume that you get past that. You can create a name and a logo, and all that can be registered. You will then have to go out and persuade others. You may provide it at low or no cost to a couple of ice cream stores, where they build sundaes. You ask them if they would be willing to make it a flavor of the week - that kind of stuff. You hopefully can persuade storekeepers and even the ice cream stores to sell it on a take-home basis just to see if it gains some acceptance. If it gets acceptance in a small market, then you may have something to sell to a manufacturer.

You cannot make stuff for public consumption on your private stove unless you want to invest a huge amount of money and go through the health approvals etc. If I were doing it, I would do it on a very casual basis. Invite people to your home for a tasting. That will be covered by your homeowner's insurance, I think. As soon as you put it out for money, you have to have product liability insurance, a license and so on and so forth.

Have an ice cream social - play games, etc. In terms of getting the costs down, you may be able to cut a deal with a local ice cream parlor, a place that does their own ice creams and top-pings, to go into a partnership. They have the facility, it's licensed, etc. and it is already in place with no expenditure on your part except in parting with the formula. That would cut the expenses down dramatically.

A caution though, the last place you want to cut costs is with your ingredients. I have to believe that your mother used the best that she could find. That may contribute to the flavor. Of course, after you go downrange you may find some economies. I would not make those economies at this time. I would want "Rolls Royce" ingredients.

Now, once you get past the acceptance of your little group, then you have to start talking about money. It is not easy. That is why a partnership with somebody already working in the ice cream business may be something you want to think about.

What can I do about a company that has tricked my husband out of our life savings?

This company is supposed to send him names of customers to send their product to, but first my husband has to pay C.O.D. for the product. The names either never come, or the few that do never buy. How can I get him out of this?

■First of all, it is clear that your husband is not filling orders or even selling the product, he is buying it. Why do you suppose that they need him if they have orders? Why don't they just fill the orders themselves? What you're describing is a multi-level marketing scheme. I'll bet it's out of state and shipped UPS. They would not use the mail.

In my opinion you have been defrauded. The products probably don't do what they are claiming and they have not sent you the list of names to supply product to - the orders.

I would talk to my local District Attorney. If the fellows who originally called are out of state it will be much harder to get them. The District Attorney may be able to make a phone call to the area where the company is located. There is interstate commerce involved here. Ask him how to direct you. Whether or not a civil action would be appropriate, I do not know. I wish I had a better answer for you. I think you have been stuck.

CHAPTER 8 *Career-Employment*

" You are never going to be a successful boss if you're trying to win a popularity contest. "

How do I choose between a career as a veterinarian or a zoologist?

I'm a freshman in a community college and I am not so much interested in treating animals myself as in teaching people how to take care of their own animals.

■I think most people would agree that the veterinarian profession is overcrowded right now. Zoology is a pretty broad field, but if you're going to college to learn how to earn a living, I believe that you have to be a tad more realistic in terms of the marketability of your skills. Zoology is certainly not the kind of job where you pick up the classified section and look under "Zoologists Wanted". It's just not going to happen.

College has many facets, not the least of which is to prepare you to make a living.

How do I beat the prejudice against youth in the financial field?

I'm a 25 year old college graduate with a degree in business. I'm looking for a position as a stockbroker. I'm getting turned down because they want someone with more experience.

■You are going to find a degree of prejudice because of your age as well as your inexperience, but there are lots of people your age who are customers. So if you're not afraid of cold-calling and you really want to be a customer's man, there's a brokerage firm out there that is going to hire you.

The question is how badly do you want it? If it's very badly, there are more offices out there than you can possibly try. The fact that you have been turned down by firm "A" once doesn't mean that you don't go back there. If I were you I would go back ten times to the same firm. A prime requisite for any sales person is persistence. So what do you have to lose?

Am I nuts to go with a job I like that pays a lot less money than the job I have now?

I really don't like the corporate life. I got an offer for a lot less money - from $32,000 down to $18,000. There is potential for more, but I'm hesitating. Right now I have a very good job with a very large company, but I hate it. I am single, 35, with no debts and no children.

■So you don't like that corporate scene - the regulation tie, regulation suit, regulation uniform...all that good stuff? Look, it sounds to me like you're in a position to make your move - no heavy responsibilities to tie you down. You can try out the new position and if it isn't what you had hoped, you should have enough to keep you in groceries for a limited time to find something else.

What's holding you back? Tomorrow is the first day of the rest of your life.

Is correspondence school a reasonable alternative to college?

I want to enroll in a correspondence school to study bookkeeping or accounting. I'm in my thirties, divorced with two kids and no time to go back to college. I have no help with the kids. I do not qualify for federal programs because my income is not low enough.

■I'm not going to tell you that I would not consider a correspondence school, but I would give a lot of thought to trying to find something with an on-campus curriculum someplace in your area.

To help with the little ones, you may want to consider running an ad to share child care with other women in the neighborhood while you're going to school. I understand that the children's welfare is your primary concern. I also understand that it costs money. You may be able to find another lady with kids who has the same custodial problem and swap times with her. You could take care of kids for other mothers in exchange for care for your children while you go to school. That way there are no dollars flying out.

It is hard for me to believe that you could not find the kind of courses that you are looking for at community colleges, and pay less money and probably accelerate your training.

That makes more sense to me than the correspondence approach.

There are also on-the-job training programs that you may want to investigate.

Should I try to find a job on my own or go to a career counselor or head-hunter?

I own my business, but I'm feeling burned out fighting the daily ups and downs. Where do I go to find out what my marketable skills are or how they would be applied?

■You could market yourself like anybody else looking for a job. I'm not certain that you need to sign up with an agency. You have certain skills. The first thing you do is take an inventory of those skills, write them down, then figure out who needs those skills and present yourself to those people. Knock on the door, send them a letter, set up an appointment, etc. You need to have a good answer as to why you do not want to be in business for yourself anymore. It is one of the first questions they will ask you. If you're so good why do you want to come to work for me?

Let's start with the premise that you're the toughest guy in the world to find a job for. The reason for that is fairly apparent: people who have owned their own business are frequently not the best employees. The problem is that you are accustomed to being the boss and if a decision had to be made, you made it. You did not have to have a committee meeting, didn't have to worry about writing a memo on it. You got the job done - rightly or wrongly. That is the joy and sorrow of owning your own enterprise. Most people in business recognize that the people who have done that for a significant period of time are not the best employees in the world.

Am I too old to go into business for myself?

I'm 43 years old and Vice President of a major corporation in their marketing department. I've had enough of corporate politics and I'm tired of seeing my contemporaries, who, through no fault of their own, have gotten their careers knocked out from under them because of corporate acquisitions.

■If you are too old at 43, I'm really in trouble. Look, if you don't have the vim and vigor you had twenty years ago, hopefully you have more smarts. And if you don't, you have a serious problem.

Before you venture outside the corporate walls, there are some fundamental things to get past here. You have been a corporate animal for the last two decades and my experience tells me that it is quite different from being an entrepreneurial type. This is not to say that you cannot apply the skill from one to the other. It is different. Very different. Good managers of the world are seldom the good entrepreneurs of the world. What happens is entrepreneurs get knocked out when their own companies reach a certain size...by the managers. That is the way it should be because they are not up to the job. The first thing you have to determine is, are you?

Your age can work against you in your present environment. In the corporate world when they start merging and digesting people, you would be a prime candidate. You are not in a high enough place.

If you have some staying power - enough to keep you in groceries for a year, then all you're risking by trying it is time. Develop a business plan that will make sense to an investor. If you feel you're limited in the field you've chosen, you ought to get some first hand information about it. The proper deal will come along.

How do you overcome preconceptions about age in certain jobs?

I have worked in broadcasting for twenty two years - mostly on-air - music and talk radio for the last eight years. I have been out of work for about ten months and I'm having a tough time finding something. It seems that most people judge you by what you look like instead of what you sound like.

■When you don't get the job, it's easy to sluff it off by saying I'm too old, I'm fat, the wrong race or whatever. Sometimes you just do not have what it takes. You may not be good at it. That is a fact. You should always entertain the possibility that there is something lacking in the product that you are offering. Think about it honestly, then proceed.

As far as music formats - many of the music shows are looking for younger people because they identify more closely with that young demographic. If you are going to get into Top 40, you may be a little over the hill, but if you are talking about the big band sounds, you are right there. Let's face it, there are a couple of nationally known jocks who would make you look like a kid. Of the people who are on national talk shows right now, very few are under 50.

Look for a position that really makes sense for you - that makes use of your best qualities and talents. Then go sell yourself...and be persistent!

What's the best way to prepare for a career as a pilot?

I'm 24 years old, single and in good health. I have had only one year of college and that was a nine month machine shop course. I am interested in going into something with more of a future.

■First I would check to see if your current eyesight can get you past the appropriate examinations. Talk to an opthamologist about the likelyhood of your eyes staying in good condition. If they deteriorate between now and the time you get the appropriate tickets, you will have a problem. Don't invest a lot of money and then find out you are not going any place because you cannot pass the physicals.

There are openings for pilots. The problem is that you have to look ahead to when you can get trained. Another factor is most airlines want a college degree as well as the flying credentials and that is four years away for you.

Here's what I would do. Go out and get your private ticket, your CFI, (Certified Flight Instructor) and your various ratings. You also have to build up time. The only way the average person can build up time is get a CFI and then teach others to fly. You get credit for the time when you are teaching them. Secondly you go to school and earn the degree. Even the corporations are asking for them. If you get your CFI, you can make enough money to support yourself while you go to school.

Also, you have to consider that your locale may not be the place to be a CFI. Why? You want to be somewhere where the weather is more conducive to flying because you only get paid when you are in the air and you want to be somewhere where there is decent flying weather a better part of the year. Consider the local economy, private flying may be considered too much of a luxury. Commercial flying is another matter. The average person who is getting his ticket is doing it for kicks. I want you to go out and substantiate everything that I have told you, but I think you will find it fairly accurate.

How can I help my son get into the Air Force Academy?

He's a junior in high school with a solid 3.5 grade point average. He's a good athlete, not outstanding, but a good football player. He has all the applications now and I need some advice on how to help in getting accepted. Also, since he has put in his application to the Air Force Academy he has gotten several letters from other places. The Navy sent him an R.O.T.C. deal.

■First, you ought to be contacting your congressman. There are congressional appointments, but they're very competitive. You say he's an athlete. They are looking for good athletes, but he needs to be outstanding in sports. That is the calibre of athlete they are looking for to get that type of scholarship.

Tell him to keep the GPA up. That is important. Sometimes they assign an officer in the area to get acquainted with an applicant. I do not know if that is still in operation today.

There is a vast difference between a military college like the Air Force Academy and an ROTC campus. If you've visited college campuses, you do not have to be very perceptive to see the difference. I would have no reservations about sending a son of mine to a military academy, assuming that is what he wants to do. This is not an ordinary college experience. But, if you wanted the best academic education, you could probably do as well or better in ROTC at one of the finer universities.

Is there security in a career in the financial industry?

What I have been looking into is the financial market. Could you give me a few insights on what you think it will be in the 1990s. I have been reading things that say if there is a crash a lot of the people that are making over $100,000 will end up driving taxis.

■If you are asking me if there is money to be made in the financial area, there is an ocean to be made. The problem is that it requires a great deal of effort. This is not a thirty five or forty hour week job we are talking about. We are talking about seventy to ninety hours a week.

It may be true that a crash can bring a lot of people down. But what field are you going to go into that is not going to be affected by a crash? In a less severe scenerio, the broker makes money both buying and selling. Bulls make money and bears make money. There will always be prophets of doom with us. There is much more money to be made saying things are going to hell than predicting we're all going to live happily ever after.

Should I put in an extra semester to get an accounting degree in addition to a finance degree?

Some people are saying accounting is a waste because soon it will all be computerized.

■I would go the extra semester and get both degrees. You can not have enough bullets in your gun. For one short semester of work it's worth it to have the dual competency.

Would you suggest that I finish my Bachelor's Degree before trying to change jobs?

I've been an electronics technician for the past fourteen years making good money, but I'm not happy with my job. I would probably like to stay in a technical area - perhaps in computer or technical equipment sales. I have two years sale's experience. Also, is 32 a good age to be changing careers?

■A degree is necessary to wipe the windows. It's a fact. It's just paying your dues and you're not in that great a rush are you? I would get the degree and at the same time start finding out what potential employers are looking for.

I don't know if there is a bad age to change careers. First of all 32 is young. To put it another way, you have thirty-odd years ahead of you if we are going to adopt sixty five as the year for retirement. If you are unhappy in what you are doing, I don't care if you are making a million bucks a year, you are underpaid.

So, you said you think you'd like to stay in the technical area and perhaps sales. There are two distinct kinds of sales - retail and wholesale.

In retail, there are people making good money. That does not mean that you are going to make it. It is not for everybody, certainly. When you were selling, were you comfortable?

Now it is one thing to sell to the public - that's retail. It is another to represent a company and try to sell products to stores - wholesale. That is a different kind of selling. One of the things you can bring to this marriage, and it would seem to me a rather important commodity, is that you can address the technical questions that a potential retailer or his buyer might want to ask. That is a strength that the average salesman would not have. He can parrot back a little bit about the technical end, but when customers ask about resistance and all the component parts, the average salesperson is lost.

The retail customer is not going to have the need for the depth of information that you can get into. Given that, don't you think it is a waste of your background to work at the retail level? You would be better utilized, it would seem to me, at the wholesale

Is it a mistake to force myself to look for a job by quiting my present job first?

I want to find a new job. I want to nail it down before I quit my present job, but it's so easy just to keep working here. I'm wondering if I should quit, just to put the pressure on myself to make the move.

■It is a turn off when you are applying for a job and you convey the idea that, "I will do anything, go anyplace, to get the job." So someone who is employed is generally a better job seeker than someone who is not.

Having time to contact employers on a relatively leisurely basis, rather than in desperation, is a big asset when you are applying for a job.

How can I improve my performance selling real estate?

I got my real estate license about six weeks ago and I have not had very much success in the business so far. We don't get much traffic through the door. I have floor duty in the afternoons. I've gone out on the streets knocking on doors, looking for residential listings, but I don't have my cards yet so I just write my name on blank company cards.

■If you are in a live office and there is nobody walking through the door as a result of advertising, something is wrong. One of several things is happening - either the real estate market is really lousy where you are, the office is not advertising properly, or somebody is grabbing the cream before you see it.

The worst time for floor duty is in the afternoon. Weekends are when you get the most activity because that is when people are looking for houses. The last thing I would do is write my name on business cards. You can get business cards printed in twelve hours. Walk into one of these instant places and they will knock them out for you the same day. We are talking about transactions for tens of thousands of dollars. Are you inspired by someone who hands you a thing where they write their name on a blank card or fill their name in? I want to know that I am dealing with somebody of substance and permanence. I think you are wasting your time writing your name on a business card.

There is money in getting listings. In fact there is probably more money if you are really good at it. Get those cards printed and go knock on doors. Getting listings, by and large, is an arduous thing and a lot of it comes from networking and people saying, "I called Harry and the house moved in two weeks." That kind of stuff.

It is a tough business. It takes time to generate contacts, time to make a sale, and time for the money to get through the pipeline. But, if there is advertising, somebody ought to be calling and coming in and you should have a shot at getting them.

But, again, if you are not getting walk-ins, I would look for a new agency. It does not sound to me like it is a very lively place. How many million dollar producers do you have in your office? Check that out.

level. There are some things you can do there also. Some companies have a technician who services the existing accounts - who goes out and discusses problems with the buyers and their sales people. Maybe there is a niche for you in there some place.

Is the military a good choice for someone with a college degree?

I have a wife and child and a degree in geology and I'm having a tough time finding a job. I'm told that being an officer in the military is a good thing to get into right now.

■It might be a good idea. There is nothing wrong with that. The pay is decent. There is a future there. The oil crisis has become a reality and geologists are not in heavy demand. Unfortunately, geology is a field that is dead right now. I do not know how else to put that. That's nobody's fault and it will change. In the meantime, I would go out and get some new skills. I don't see where your degree will take you very far right now.

What's the best way to approach job hunting?

I am thinking about sending some resumes out, but I've heard you say resumes are not the best way to go about it.

■No, I probably said resumes are the worst way to go about it. First, I would be looking into companies whose circumstances could be enhanced by your experience and talents. Consider what companies you could make a difference in...that is, help them make more money.

Do your homework. Say you are going to go after **NBC Radio**. You would want to find out who in that company is involved in your area of expertise. That is the person you are going to write to. You ought to know something about **NBC Radio** when you write the letter - like the fact that it is owned by **Westwood One**, it has been in business for so many years, these are the products they are producing, and so on and so forth.

Rather than sending a resume, you are going to write to an individual. That in itself sets you apart. What do you suppose the average guy does with a resume? He throws it away. I would. I get them all the time and do not read them. I have more things to do with my time than read a resume. If you send me a one page letter, you've got a shot at me. But one page is all you are going to get out of me... and it better be double spaced. I read the letters to the editor in the newspaper regularly. I do not read the long ones, only the short ones. You have to be brief. One page, double spaced is what you need to do.

Do I need more education?

I'm 26 years old, in the military and trying to decide whether to stay in and let them pay for school, creating a commitment to them, or strike out on my own and see if I can get an employer to pay for my education.

■It is not at all uncommon for industry or the military to subsidize an education, but who is really paying for it? As an example...if you stay in the military, while they're "paying" for your education, it is possible that you will be earning less than you might be in a comparable civilian occupation. You're earning that education then, aren't you? You're earning it by the commitment that you give to the military, to our country, and getting less money in your paycheck every week.

If you pay it out of your own pocket, you are giving up something too. You're giving up your time. And that cannot be replaced. As I see it, there is nothing free. Not even your education.

The first thing you need to determine is where you want to be in five, ten or fifteen years. That is a terrible question to ask at twenty six. Who knows, you may change and do four or five career flips between now and the time you're thirty five and there is certainly nothing wrong with that, despite what some people will tell you. You have to focus and forget all the nonsense.

I have a tremendous faith in my gut reactions. If you have gut feelings, go for it. The kind of gal or guy who wants that degree should get it. I never wanted a Ph.D., but I found out that you have to have a degree, otherwise no one wants to talk to you, so I went back and paid my dues. I would go for it, but that is me, and that does not make it right for you.

My inclination would be to get the education outside of the military, where you would have a little less restriction placed on you. I would go for it full-time, okay? You mentioned that you were married with kids and some would say that full time school cannot be done. It can. I went down that street already.

There is no free lunch. The subsidy is an extra that you are paying for, whether you use it or not. It is earned by putting time in the military. They say education is free in California. It is not free, you pay taxes. More taxes than you pay in Florida. So how is that free? Free is an illusion.

Can a person be successful without going to college?

I would like to go to college. Because I'm good in math, people have advised me to major in economics. I'm 23 with a high school education. Do you believe that college degrees translate into bucks? I read about people who have made millions without cracking a book.

■If I were advising you, I would tell you to go back to school with an undeclared major. That means that you go back and you don't pick a major right now. Rather than try to focus on a degree program, you take general courses. You'll be exposed to all kinds of academic disciplines - things that you don't know exist right now. Then at the end of your sophomore year you pick your major, which could be economics. But go back with an open mind.

If you are going to go for any kind of a Liberal Arts degree, you are going to have to take certain basic courses - English courses, writing courses, probably a math course, a statistics course, some of the sciences, whatever, right? I am saying get rid of this in your freshman and sophomore years as much as you are able to, and kind of keep your eyes and ears open. Then make your decision two years from now. Really, if you talk with your guidance counselor at the school of your choice, I think you are going to find that that's his opinion also.

And do I believe that a degree translates into bucks? Do I believe the sun comes up in the east? There are stories about people who never cracked a book and have made tons of money. There are always those stories. But, why do they write articles about them? Because they're unusual.

I know a fellow in his seventies - he'll kill me for talking about him - he was one child in a large farm family and I think when he was in the fourth grade the school sent him home. They said, "Look, he's a nice kid but he's never going to make it, certainly not in school. Put him back on the farm." Well, the school teacher should be around today to see this guy. He owns, I think, the biggest enterprise in the state of it's kind. He is the exception to the rule. And as times goes on, your generation is going to find it tougher and tougher to make it without the academic preparation.

I was the wise guy. I was a hot shot. When I was 23, I didn't have time for college. I was in a big hurry, right? I had to wait until I was a freshman at 25 to smarten up. I didn't graduate until I was 29 and had three kids.

It would have been a whole lot smarter to go on from high school to college, skip the war, go play football the way they wanted me to, and get out when I was 22. The war would have been gone. But that's not the way I did it you see. I was the wise guy. I was industrial strength stupid and I paid for that. Now you aren't very bright either. You are 23 and you haven't gone to school yet. Okay, that's history.

Now, having said all that, let me also say that there's absolutely no disgrace in not going to college. There is a whole bunch of money made in the trades. I mean good plumbers are paid a lot of dough. Pipe fitters and all the other trades are paid well, too. But, I am saying, if you are academically oriented - if you have the smarts - you'll find it worth your while to go for it.

For every one of those guys who didn't get through high school and makes 40-million dollars, there are 40-million guys that don't make forty cents.

Would it be a mistake for me to restrict myself to a Special Education Certificate?

I'm 45 years old and I need to really be sure that I'm going in the right direction toward a generic Special Ed Certificate. The certificate simply qualifies me to teach those students who are determined to have special needs.

■I think you are going to find there are many more employment opportunities in Special-Ed than there are in the regular areas. That has been the case certainly for the last quarter of a century, and I don't see it changing. And there is nothing to say that you can't go on and get certified in other areas as well.

I have a dual certification. That was the norm when I was going to school. There is no reason why you can't do that also.

I don't think mainstreaming means doing away with special ed teachers. And if you understand what mainstreaming entails, you know doggone well that these children, with many different difficulties, cannot be stuck in the classroom in every situation. Mainstreaming in education, for those unfamiliar with the term, is putting kids back into the regular classroom for those activities which they can handle. As an example, you might have a youngster who has a heavy-duty disability, but he can work out just fine in a physical ed class. You put him in a normal physical ed. class. Or he can do just great in the band because he can handle that. So you give him normal band, etc. But, in those areas where he has a problem, you put him in special ed and you don't let him fail in classes where he shouldn't be. You give him the special help he needs. That's all mainstreaming is, and I believe people like yourself will always be necessary.

So all I am saying to you is, I think Special Education is an area that you have to be attuned to. Some people can handle it and some cannot. I think you could make the same statement for people who work in geriatrics. It takes a very special person to walk in and work with people who are in the various conditions you find in nursing homes. The same thing is true for working with the retarded, where you need specialized experience. You also need special training to work with the hearing disabled. But, basically, it takes the ability to empathize - to understand. If you don't have it, you don't belong in the field.

Can my employer terminate me arbitrarily and not be in violation of my employment contract?

One paragraph states that I can be terminated for demonstrating a lack of ability to do the job in the opinion of the Board of Directors of the company. Included in this section is being drunk, mental and-or physical illness rendering the employee unable to perform the job. My attorney said the specifics encompass the parameters of the quarrel. I took that to mean that the reason for termination on this point would be physical or mental disability.

■It looks to me like the first paragraph gives them the right to say that you are not doing the job. It gives them the opportunity to let you go at anytime. But, I cannot interpret it better than your attorney because I do not have it in front of me and I would not do that anyway. I see it a little broader than that.

Consult an attorney who feels he can defend your position. That is the trick for an attorney. It doesn't matter what he believes, he has to be able to defend the position his client adopts. You tell him what position it is and that is the position he should defend.

How can I get my four-man crew to treat me like a boss and forget I'm a woman?

They don't like having a woman for a boss and it's gotten to where they won't do work that I schedule for them on time. The president of the company tells me not to be so hard on them, try to be more "feminine", try and be their "buddy". I want to be liked, but it's more important to get the job done, right? I'm so frustrated I'm about to quit.

■If these guys cannot accept a supervisor who happens to be a female, then you have to be strong enough to say, "I do not know how we will get along without you on Monday, but we are going to make a strong effort."

After you issue a warning, if you have to fire one of them, make certain that you fire him on very firm grounds. You say, "Look, I'm giving you fair warning. Nobody goes home until this job is done. It is now three pm, Friday. The job is only worth maybe forty-five minutes, so at four o'clock I expect that it will be done. If it is not done, on Monday morning we are going down to Union Hall and replace you." You have to set the parameters. If you pick up your marbles and go home, all you are doing is going along with their nonsense.

You are never going to be a successful boss if you're trying to win a popularity contest. I do not want to see a woman get the slightest concession because of her gender. The reason is, if you get concessions because you're a woman, you are also going to be discriminated against because you're a woman. You cannot have it both ways.

Should I make phony expense reports at my boss's request in order to make up for income that cannot be listed as a raise?

I'm a sales rep for a national company. I make $37,000 a year with commissions. The company wants to double my territory, but they can't raise my compensation more than 7% a year. I just don't know how I feel about doing bogus expense reports.

■As long as your boss authorizes this - and I would want it in writing - I'd go along with it. But I wouldn't try to bury the thing. Be up front and consistent. Every week turn in for the same thing.

This is a pretty common way of getting around company policy. They can't give you a raise commensurate with your new responsibility, so they'll give you a fringe of some kind. If you tell me it's not especially moral, how can I argue with you? Who was it, Sam Rayburn?...Said "To get along, you got to go along." Politics is the art of compromise, and corporate politics is still politics...

CHAPTER 9 *Cars*

" You not only borrowed the dollar to buy the car, you borrowed the interest too. " "

How do I get replacement value for a car that was totaled in an accident?

I have an older car, so there's no Blue Book value for it. My insurance agent told me that, even though I have a lot of money into it, I probably will not get very much for it. The lady who pulled out in front of me admitted that it was her fault. I want to be able to buy another car just like it. Also, is her insurance company responsible for providing me with a rental car?

■Unfortunately, you won't get much for your car. I wish there was a way you could get it replaced with one just like it, but that just does not work. Her responsibility to you is to reimburse you, assuming that they (the insurance company) want to accept full responsibility. They could say sue us. And they would not have to pay you a nickel until you sue them and win.

But, making the assumption that they say, "Okay, our insured was wrong and we are going to settle this matter," I cannot see them going more than the market value of the car - what you would have to pay for that model and year car. Now others may not be in as good a shape as your car, I understand all that. But everybody with an older car, maybe justifiably, feels it is worth more than the average because it may have been rejuvenated with new parts, extra goodies and a lot of TLC. That argument will fly a little bit but not too terribly far.

Her admitted guilt has nothing to do with anything. Let's assume that she was wrong. She may very well allege contributory negligence, which means you are partially responsible. I am not going to tell you this is right or wrong, but if I were the other guy, it would be my position. The fact that you were there is a contributing factor. In most cases they are not responsible for providing you with a rental car.

Can an auto dealer change the finance agreement on a new car after everybody has signed it and I've driven the car home?

I bought a new car over the weekend. The dealership called Monday and said they made a mistake and need to charge me about 2% more. They've already wholesaled my trade-in, so I couldn't even take it back. I felt like we had a contract and that I am right in sticking to it. I just don't think this is the way to do business.

■I don't either. I do not understand how they can let you take the car home, sell your trade-in, and then change the financing after the fact.

I could be totally off base, but if I went down on Thursday and bought a car at 10% financing and they took my car in trade and gave me the new car, put it in my name, etc., then the following Tuesday told me that the rates had gone up, they would have to prove to me in court that their position is defensible.

Is a threat to safety reason enough to get out of an auto lease?

I leased a car with a dangerous problem the dealer can't seem to fix no matter how many times I take it back. The Attorney General's office says the Lemon Law applies only to the owner of the car, which is the leasing company.

■There are a lot of ways you can get out of a lease. We are talking in general terms now. Obviously, your attorney would have the benefit of having your lease in front of him, but let's talk in very general terms and please take exception to what I am going to say if you see a flaw.

A lease is nothing more and nothing less than a contract between two parties. They agree to provide and you agree to pay for and so on and so forth. Well one of the things they agree to provide is a safe automobile, a functioning automobile. Your position is, I am willing to pay but you have not provided a safely operating automobile. As a consequence, you've abrogated this contract and I consider it null and void. Now your attorney has to defend that position. But it seems to me that it is a defensible position.

What can I do after having bought a used car that was sold to me as a demonstrator?

I brought the vehicle in for repair and the service manager told me the service contract says it's used - the dealership had leased the car to someone before I bought it. The car had 6,000 miles when I got it.

■I would go to an attorney and bring a civil action against them for fraud and if they wouldn't deal with me, I'd file a criminal action against them. Make a complaint with the District Attorney or your city prosecutor. The dealer defrauded you, pure and simple.

A "demonstrator" is a vehicle that a salesman has used. It's not a question of using it for demonstration. It is a legitimate fringe benefit for him. But you're telling me that this car was out of their care and custody, that they leased it to somebody and brought it back in again. That makes it a used car.

How can I increase the insurance settlement on my totaled car?

The leasing company is saying that I owe them $1,300 more than the insurance company will pay on 100% collision coverage. I was forced to buy another car. They didn't give me any options.

■I do not know what your rights are here. They are spelled out in the lease. Before I paid them any money, I would have an attorney review it. It seems reasonable to me that they have a responsibility to replace your car and continue on with your original lease agreement. But, that may not be the case.

What they are saying is, as is frequently the case in a finance or lease environment, the car is not worth what is owed on it. That is not unusual. The point is, under a lease, I just don't know how that would be treated.

Will my insurance pay off my previously-damaged car for a later accident in which it was totaled?

Last week my girlfriend was hit while driving my four year old Nissan. The insurance company said the car was a total loss. The car already had about $1,500 worth of damage in the front from another accident. It was paid off, but I didn't get the repairs done. I still owe about $2,000 on it. What if the insurance company gives me less?

■The value of the car would be depreciated by the amount of the first accident. It's called "O.D." or old damage. They deduct for mileage, too...if it's above average mileage they will knock off more. You should receive the average market value unless there is something to indicate that the car was in bad shape or the car was in extraordinary good shape.

Not repairing the previous damage is in violation of your contract with the financing company. If you damage their collateral - your car - you are supposed to get it fixed. That amount comes off the top because you did not have the work done. The front end was not worth what the front end of a four year-old Nissan would ordinarily be worth.

If the insurance company decides to pay you less than you owe the finance company, you will have to pay the difference. You should have used that $1,500 they paid you for the damage to bring the car up to full value. You will not collect twice, and you may owe them money.

Can I trade one car in for a less expensive one with lower payments and not lose a lot of money?

A few months ago I purchased an expensive car. Well, my eyes were bigger than my wallet and now I am finding it difficult to make the payments.

■You will lose money trading in a new car you've had only a short time. When you buy a new car and drive it out the door, in almost every instance, it is worth less than it was before you drove it home.

To further compound this situation, if you look at the paperwork with your loan, I think you will find someplace in there where it says that this interest is computed under the rule of 78's. That means that you not only borrowed the dollars to buy the car, you borrowed the interest too.

There is a strong possibility that since you have owned this car only a short time you owe more on it than you borrowed. On top of that, the car now is probably worth only 60% of what you paid for it.

The break even point is probably about two years into the contract. You are stuck with it.

How do you sell a classic car and what is a fair price?

My husband passed away two months ago and this was his car. It's a 1970 Cadillac Eldorado. It's a two-time trophy winner in excellent shape.

■There are a number of places where you can advertise a car of that kind. There is Hemmings Motor News out of Bennington, Vermont which is the biggest automobile magazine in the country.

You must determine what the car is worth. There are many experts around the country who could handle that for you. But first, the one thing you need to do is look at Hemmings. You will see cars advertised, and you can also advertise there as well. I would never advertise a classic car in a local auto seller publication because you need a bigger audience in a more cosmopolitan city for that type of car. Major newspapers, such as New York Times, have columns that are widely used and read. Start watching those columns and see what prices people are asking for similar automobiles. There are also classic dealers - you can call them. They take the car, appraise it and then sell it for a commission. In other cases they sometimes buy outright. Again, look in the New York Times and check out other larger city papers for classic dealers. If it were me, I would be more comfortable with the commission end. You get a piece of the action. That takes the burden off you.

How would I go about determining the value of a vintage automobile I am considering buying?

The one that I have in mind is a 1939 Rolls-Royce. It is right-hand drive. Would you have any reservations about purchasing this automobile through an automobile auction?

■Hemmings Motor News, a magazine published in Vermont, is the bible of the antique car business. Check with them. There are also dealers with whom you can consult - you should be able to find them in this same publication.

There are plenty of auctions I would go to, but I would find out what I was buying. And like everything else, it depends on who you are buying from. I would have a good idea of what I was prepared to pay and not pay any more. That is the danger of an auction and the fun of an auction.

Rolls-Royces can vary dramatically. The condition, type of engine, etc. Right hand drive is worth less than left hand drive.

Am I responsible to repair a car that I sold to another party?

The car is still in my possession until she pays the remaining half of the purchase price. Occasionally I go out and start the car, just to keep it charged, and I smelled something burning. My mechanic said it was the air conditioning condenser and it would cost about $400 to fix. According to our contract, she should have paid it off by now.

■I think that you are on very shaky ground. The car should have passed to her by now according to your agreement, at such event you would have been off the hook.

I would never have gone near the car. Once that car was sold on paper I would have parked it and never moved it.

Technically it seems to me that it is her problem, morally, I don't know. I might give her half toward the condenser, just to be done with it.

How can I contact some people who have defrauded me in the sale of a car?

*I purchased what I thought was a low mileage car. I was inform-
ed by the state that the title had been tampered with and actually
the odometer was rolled back about 70,000 miles. They also informed me that I'm entitled to three times the damages. I have
the address of the children of the people named on the title, but
not their parent's name. I'm afraid to just walk up to the door
because they would recognize me as the person who bought the
car.*

■Go look at the mailbox. Or go next door. I'm sure the
neighbors would know their name.

You could get their account number from your cancelled check.
The next step would be to go to the District Attorney. Unless you
can contact them and come to a conclusion file a criminal complaint against them.

The seat in my new car is very uncomfortable. How can I get the dealer to either exchange the seat or the car?

*It has a 13-way power seat. You can adjust it to just about every
position, but none that is comfortable for me. It's killing my
lower back. All I want to do is get other seats. I would take
another car or whatever. They have none of those models left.
They said I'd have to trade-in my two month old car on the next
year's model.*

■I'd try a cushion. If you need to, have it custom made for
your back. It would be cheaper than losing all that money trading
in a new car. I'd never trade in a new car because of an uncom-
fortable seat. It's hard to believe you cannot find an agreeable
position on a 13-way adjustable seat. You should be able to get
that seat into the same position as a bench seat.

How can I convince a car dealer that my year-old car has defective paint?

When the car had 3,000 miles on it, the dealer repainted the lower quarter panel because of peeling. He also put on a plastic coating. Now the same problem is occuring again. This time there's some chipping. He says something, like gravel, must be hitting it.

■It is a paint defect in my opinion. Go find an expert out there. The fellows that operate paint shops are experts. Have one of them take a look at it and give you his opinion - in writing. Then take that to your dealer. But, until you have an expert examine the problem, any opinion is simply speculation.

How can I get my car repaired satisfactorily after an accident?

After the initial repair job I noticed some unnatural tire wear. I took it to another mechanic and he said the frame was bent. The insurance company's repair shop has tried three times now, but I still have the same problem. I took it to a frame shop. They said it was bent and would cost $400 to fix it. I'm concerned that the insurance company thinks it's all fixed and won't pay any more.

■It's not uncommon for a car to have hidden damages as the result of a collision. It's the kind of thing that doesn't always show up when you take the car in for an estimate. They check it all over, but frequently when they tear the car down, there are other damages. Not uncommon. You are entitled to have that corrected. If your insurance company picked the repair shop, it's their problem.

You see, we don't really know what the problem is, exactly. Maybe the frame shop doesn't know what they are talking about. The liklihood is that they do, but we do not know that. I would dump it back on the insurance company's lap. Give them a copy of the estimate for the bent frame.

I don't think you have a whole lot to worry about. You may have a little hassle though.

Do I have any recourse against the manufacturer of my car for a malfunction that caused an accident?

The car suddenly accelerated with no warning and I ended up going through a brick wall. The brakes didn't stop it. It's a two year old car. The dealer says there is nothing wrong with the accelerator. I had collision coverage, so insurance is paying for the whole thing. The adjuster said there is nothing wrong with the accelerator. But, I definitely had my foot on the brake.

■I would let the insurance company go after the manufacturer. Without being able to prove a defect, you're out of business.

It may have been a problem with the cruise control. It is tied into your acceleration system and it might have been a cruise control problem.

What percentage of my income should I spend on a vehicle?

Is there a percentage rule? What would you recommend for someone who makes $35,000 per year? I use the car to go to and from work. I'm just an average guy...no dependents, single, a few credit cards. I'm renting for $450 a month.

■A percentage formula would work only to a point. It depends on your income. If you're making $100,000 a year, 10% won't kill you. If you're making ten thousand, it might.

Let's look at the whole situation. You're single now, but will you remain that way? This is also something you need to consider. All these factors have a bearing on the whole. Very low rent, $35,000 gross a year. Go out and buy a car for $12,000 to $15,000. You have no other major obligations so you can handle it.

Is it worth sueing a dealer because he sold me an '85 when I thought it was an '86?

I trade my cars in about every year or so. I get a discount from the company I work for. I went to trade this vehicle in and was told the truck was an older vintage than I thought I had purchased. The title come back saying 1985. The dealer says it was a typist's error. They won't do anything about it.

■You need to talk to someone in your company. You are in a better position than most of us because you work there. I think you have been beat. If they agreed to deliver an '86 and gave you an '85, you got a car that is worth a whole lot less money just by virtue of it's model year. Yes, I think it's worth messing with.

Let your company know that you have been had by one of the dealers. They may take a very narrow view of this and want to have a chat with their dealer. I don't know, but I would find out.

You must be kidding about trading in a car every year. I would review my buying habits. Buying a new automobile every year, even with the discounts, is hard to justify. I don't see where it makes a whole lot of sense.

Are classic car kits worth the money?

I'm thinking of it as an investment. They wanted something like $6,000 in kit form.

■I would stay away from them. If you do mess with them, you better know what you are doing. My prejudice is showing here, but I don't like those kits worth a damn. They just do not have the value or retain the value that the originals do. I would not want my money invested in a kit.

They are kind of nice and cute when you see them on the street or that sort of thing, but there are so many originals around, why not play with the real thing? If you want an old car, get an old car.

If I am going to buy an old Bearcat, I want a real Bearcat. Not something with a stereo and twelve speakers and an automatic transmission. If I want a Model A Ford, I will buy a Model A Ford. Kits do not do it for me at all. You look in the used car section in the major Metropolitan newspapers. You're going to see that there are lots of completed kit cars that are available at reasonably attractive prices.

CHAPTER 10 *Investments*

"You got the opinion of an individual and you acted on it. I think you bought yourself a $110,000 lesson."

How does a corporation ever know how much money it has at any one time?

With stocks fluctuating so much, how does it plan ahead?

■It doesn't. You can take certain things for granted, but you have to leave a lot of room for contingencies. Let's forget about a corporation. You are an individual and you have of your money invested in equities. On any given day your net worth can jump all over the lot. That is part of the condition that exist when you are involved in equities. Now if you do not want that condition to continue, you stay liquid, you stay in cash and things like Treasury Bills - things that are non-fluctuating. They also don't return anything like what equities can return.

As a safeguard, you can employ a "stop sale." That's one way you will be assured that your stock value will never fall below a certain point - a particular security is automatically sold. As an example, suppose you had stop orders in with ten points. This means that your worth could not fall off more than 10%. I think wise investors use a "stop" when they can.

If I buy a stock and lose because of bad advice, do I have any recourse?

The manager of a major brokerage firm told me that if they reduce the margin requirments to 50%, this market is really going to roar for the next couple of weeks. On the basis of what he said I bought stocks that I could not afford and ended up losing $110,000.

■From a statutory point of view, you are dead in the water. You got the opinion of an individual and you acted on it. I think you bought yourself a $110,000 lesson.

If a brokerage house mistakenly credits my account with a lot of money, do I have to turn it back?

I placed a $4,000 order to buy on a tax free income trust fund through a brokerage house. Instead of what I ordered, they sent me a stock certificate for $40,000.

■It's not your money. Trust me, they will come after you. Send it back, it is only paper. You will go to jail. If you keep it, it's called fraud. I suggest you send it back to them.

How do I investigate a company before I invest in it?

I read Money Magazine, Fortune, Sylvia Porter's magazine, and the Wall Street Journal. But how do you get a company's individual records?

■The serious question to answer first is - are you qualified to evaluate a company? There are a number of publications, but I tell you that you are taking on a heck of a task. It is not one that I would discourage you from, but it is a heck of a task.

You can read what has been written about a particular company. Take a look at their annual reports. See what the background of the company is. You could begin at the library. Any good broker can provide a list of information about a company.

The way to find out the facts is to inquire. But this is why most major brokerage houses, discount houses excepted, have research departments. If you are interested in a particular company, you can call a full service broker. That is why people use full service brokers. In all liklihood their research department has written something on the company. Or, if they have not, they can go to one of their competitors who has written something and provide some materials for you.

Do you recommend against older people getting into the stock market?

■Unless they get a big kick out of it and can afford it, I think people in their 70s and older ought to be a little more conservative...like Treasury instruments, CDs, money market trust funds.

I suggest that because they may not be able to hang around for the market to bump up and down. If the market goes down for three or four years, they may not to be here for the raise. That's for openers. Secondly, people at that stage of life don't usually want the aggravation of losing $5,000 in one day.

Finally, oftentimes their lifestyle is severely altered if the market is disturbed. Somebody decides to cut a dividend way back...that can be pretty tough if you are depending on that income.

What legal recourse do I have if a brokerage firm charged me more commission than was originally agreed?

We purchased a mutual fund from a brokerage house, investing $32,000. It was a load fund, which means we paid a commission, and we were quoted 4 1/4%. But, when the statement came, it showed we paid 6 3/4% commission. When I asked the broker, he said there was a terrible mistake, he would look into it. He has since told us there is nothing he can do. I confirmed by phone that, yes 4 1/4 is the rate for the level of our deposit.

■Call the Compliance Office of the brokerage firm. You should have read the prospectus before buying anything. You may have a problem if the quote was verbal and not written. But, you may be correct in your assumption that the guy himself made a mistake. If he quoted you 4 1/4% that is the commission you ought to pay.

The difference, 2 1/2% of $32,000 is $620 dollars, is worth a little trouble.

What are the best investments to be looking at to give us the best yield in three to five years.

My husband and I are moving to Europe to work and we want to come back to a little more money than we left. The sale of our home should yield about $22,000 in equity and our two cars about $15,000. We're both 30 years old and can think in terms of a moderate risk level. We also have approximately $6,000 that is readily available for emergencies.

■The way you pose the question there is not an answer - the best investment. If you want the best return, you have to take some risks, don't you? But, there's always the chance that there may be nothing left when you get back to the States.

There are some rather substantial investment opportunities in Europe to that you may want to consider. There are very attractive stocks being sold in Europe. Some of those you can buy here as well, but over there people are more apt to speculate in currency. In this country, you can go 3,000 miles and you still use the dollar. You travel 3,000 miles across Europe and you hear four, five, or six languages and use half a dozen currencies.

I suspect one problem could be a difficulty keeping track of things. The easiest solution is to put the money into a diversified portfolio. I do not want to play investment advisor, but maybe a good idea would be three good mutual funds with slightly different goals...one that would be strictly for heavy duty growth, one a little more conservative, and one that was very conservatively operated. You might want to consider putting a portion in one of the metals funds as a hedge. If things go real good with the metals, the rest of the world is going to blazes.

I do not think you can afford to put the money in just an interest bearing account. And I really do not think that good stewardship would allow you to get invloved in something that requires much management because it is hard to manage from that distance. Many of the major brokerages will point out that they will have an office near you in Europe. But nonetheless, it would still require a little more stewardship than you may want to exercise.

CHAPTER 11 *Landlord-Tenant-Neighbor*

"Here's the landlord saying, 'Hey what the heck, six inches of water, get the kid a rubber duck'!"

Can I dig a trench on my neighbor's property to keep rain water from entering my basement?

I live on a hill and the neighbors above me do not have gutters. There is about a 5 foot drop from their property to mine so when it rains, I get water from their lot. I need to dig on the incline to channel the water fifty feet over to the street. In the event that I have to do this myself, do they have anything to say if I go on the hill and dig down?

■Let's separate things. You have no right to go on their property without their permission. They have no right to put water on your property. I would not do it myself. I would be very polite and tell them that there is a problem and please solve it. You are focusing on the solution. Focus on the problem. The problem is that there is water coming off of their property and flowing onto yours.

They have no right to have their water go on your property unless it is a natural flow and a flow off of a house is not considered a natural flow. If there was a stream that went through the property for the last 300 years that is one thing. It is quite another for the water to flow off the building onto your property. They have an obligation to control that, not you. The point is that the problem is his - not yours.

Call the local authorities. They may have a building inspector come out and lean on them. I believe there must be something in your building code that prohibits what they are doing.

Would we have any liability for a wall that a neighbor builds on our side of the property line?

They want to build a new wall on the outside of an old stone wall. If they do it that way, they won't have to tear the existing wall down. We feel we might be liable for repair of the wall or any injury that may occur because it's on our property.

■Well, yes and no. With injuries I don't know. It's a fine line. How do you prove that the wall caused the injury? What I would be concerned about is some future dispute about where the property line really is.

That can be remedied easily by having your attorney draw up a long-term lease for those two or three inches. For a dollar a year and other considerations, you lease them the property to put the wall on. The lease would be better than selling the land because you may have some zoning ordinances that would restrict you from reducing the size of your lot.

How do I get our neighbors to co-operate in getting rid of the cockroaches in our apartment building?

They don't even see them. I can't believe they're not in their apartment too. There is just drywall between the units. We live in a really nice duplex and we have had problems with cockroaches for about six months.

■First, capture a couple of the critters. Take them over to the university and get them to tell you what they are. Bring a professional exterminator in. I have experienced what you are talking about. In every case I brought in a professional and the problem was solved.

The problem is that if you try to exterminate them yourself, they can survive and re-infest your place. But there are some poisons that are fairly residual. I would use a pro and talk to my landlord immediately.

There is no way you are going to have them on one side and not the other. Maybe you have more groceries in your apartment. Cockroaches have to have food and moisture. In the absence of those two things, you do not have cockroaches.

How do I get a neighbor to cooperate in removing a tree that's extending onto my property?

It's at least thirty five feet over the line. The landlord said if you want to take it down, take it down. He just won't help with it. It has a lot of dead broken branches in the center that are just laying there. I mean huge branches, that are eventually going to come down either on my utility shed or into the neighbor's garage.

■The first thing I would find out is if there are local ordinances that address a problem of this kind. If they exist, the town clerk or the town solicitor can give you that information pretty quickly. Then you can have the problem handled by the local authorities.

Having said that, lets make the assumption that it is not addressed and proceed from that point. Since you have several people involved here, it might be well for each party to throw some money into the kitty and hire a local attorney to see what avenues are available to you. You could hire an attorney for an hour and a half. He or she can do some research to determine what your responsibilities and rights are and perhaps draft a letter that might stimulate this guy to do what you want done. You see, in most places you can cut the branches off, but if you damage the tree then you have a civil matter.

Unfortunately, this is a very common problem. I can think of two properties that I own where there are big trees, four feet in diameter that are near the property line and my branches extend over into the neighbor's yard. Fortunately my neighbors are not giving me any flack, and I don't know how I would handle it if they did, because I cannot imagine a tree with one side cut off of it.

Can I take a neighbor to small claims court for cutting and damaging our tree?

While we were on vacation, our neighbor cut off a branch that was touching his house from a forty-foot tree in our yard. My grandmother planted the tree years ago and now a couple of weeks after my neighbor cut it, it's dying.

■In most jurisdictions he probably had a right to cut the tree branch. But with that right came a responsibility not to damage the tree in the process. You have been deprived of a tree and I think the neighbor probably has some responsibility. That is what he has homeowner's insurance for. I suspect his liability insurance might cover this eventuality. The first thing I would do is call a tree expert to determine the condition of the tree. He'll get his stethoscope out and maybe take it's blood pressure and all that kind of stuff, put something on its tongue...whatever they do to trees...and find out if the tree really is dying. Then, assuming he says it was caused by this man's action, you get an estimate on what the tree was worth. Then you probably go to court. I think you'll find that a tree that is forty feet tall would be worth more than the small claims court threshold.

Should I take my neighbor to court to make him pay his share of bringing a sewer line up to code?

During construction work on our street the city engineer discovered my sewer line was hooked into my neighbor's before it runs down to the street. It's something that happened before I bought the house. The city has agreed to pay half the cost and I think my neighbor and I should split the rest. But he doesn't want to pay anything.

■You can always take him to court. Whether you can win or not...I don't think anyone can answer that. If the city says that you guys are in violation together, theoretically your neighbor could just seal off your sewer pipe and bring himself up to code. I think you are on very weak ground. If the city has said they'll pay half I'd go for it. You are doing real well. Get a backhoe in there and run a trench from your house down to the line, tap in and seal off the line going into his place and that's the end of it. Then decide whether or not you think it is worth pursuing in court.

How can we make one of our neighbors stop speeding down the private road we share?

There are seven of us that live along this road. We all have easements and maintain it. We have kids and pets that play along it. One of the neighbors speeds down it all the time. We've talked to him, we've posted speed limit signs, but he just ignores us. I'm afraid there's going to be an accident.

■You can put all the speed limit signs up that you want, but you cannot enforce them. And you certainly can't give out tickets because you don't have the authority. They are not being very good neighbors.

But two can play this game. There are seven neighbors that all have a right to use that road. Start parking your cars all over the road in a manner that they can't easily get past. All they can do is take you to court and that is going to cost them a great deal of inconvenience. In the meantime, they may decide that the inconvenience is not worth putting up with and maybe they ought to slow it down. I'm not going to tell you this is legal, proper or moral, but mine would be the first car parked out there.

How can we solve a shared water meter problem with our neighbor?

We live in a duplex - we own our half and an elderly lady in her 70s owns the other half. The water bill comes in her name. When we moved in we had to sign an agreement to split the bill down the middle. Now, after three and a half years she is calling to ask me how often I do my laundry, how often I flush my toilet, etc. She wants us to have our own meter and she's taken the matter to the town council. My husband wants to take her to court.

■Try calling a plumber. If you have a meter coming in on one line, it seems to me you can put a meter right next to it. What you can do is have a "Y" put in before the old meter to bring water over to your side. I don't think we are talking about a big deal. Also, your house would be more saleable with a separate meter. There is no reason to get involved in litigation. This is one you should be able to negotiate - bearing in mind that, because of her age, there is a possibility she is being a little more unreasonable because she is a little more concerned about her finances. I think it is time for you guys to be as diplomatic as you possibly can.

The last thing you want to do is go to court. That is not exactly the height of diplomacy. If you take her to court it will cost you both money. How is that smart? If you win, you lose. The only winners in a case like this are the attorneys.

How can we get our landlord to fix a leaky roof?

We have called and asked him to repair the damage, and to find where the leak is coming from, but he says there is nothing he can do about it. It is coming into my daughter's bedroom and she gets really frustrated. We get three to six inches of water all the time. We really like the place and don't want to have to move.

■If the guy just won't budge on this, maybe it's time to take some action yourself. If there's anyone in your household, a friend or whoever, who is pretty handy, I suggest you call the landlord and tell him or her that you're taking a shot at fixing this yourselves and if you're successful, you're going to charge him for it. See what he has to say. Or alternatively say, if we call a roofer and let him find the leak, we will pay him instead of paying you rent for the next month or two. But check your local landlord/tenant laws before taking this action.

It's really absurd to pay rent and live with six inches of rain in your bedroom. Here's the landlord saying, "Hey what the heck, six inches of water, get the kid a rubber duck!" I mean, that's ridiculous. You tell him, we've got to try and find the leak. You've got to do something about this or we are going to move next week. Get him off center.

Can we be evicted if we don't know where to send our rent

Six months ago our landlord disappeared and we haven't known where to send the rent. We received an eviction notice from him in the mail, but it didn't have any return address on it. And we just learned the bank is starting foreclosure proceeding on the property.

■Certainly he can evict you. You didn't pay the rent. Practically speaking, if you've made some effort to locate the guy and can't, you should put the rent in an escrow account so you can pay him when he shows up. But you ought to be looking for another place to live anyway. If the bank forecloses they are going to force you out.

Can the trustee of a family that leases me land break the lease and kick me off?

I'm a dairy farmer. My original landlord is in a rest home and his youngest daughter is named as trustee for her father. For family reasons they are trying to find a way to break the lease so that they can sell the premises and move to another area. They claim I'm letting the place go.

■A lease spells out rights, privileges, conditions and responsibilities. The question is - can they legitimately point to anything in your lease that says you are supposed to do anything that you are not doing? They have the right to collect the rent in a timely fashion. They have a responsibility to provide so many acres and so many buildings and all that sort of jazz. If in the lease it says that you will maintain the place in a clean orderly fashion then you have to do that. If it says that you have to maintain the buildings, you must do that. Now, if they can find a bunch of things that the lease says you are suppose to do that you are not doing, that would be a condition for which they can break the lease. Sit down with the lease and make certain that you are dotting all the i's and crossing all the t's. Otherwise, you may be out the door.

Should I be concerned about buying a house with a tenant still living in it?

I want to occupy the house. The tenant will be there for another three months. She has been informed of the purchase, but I have not talked to her.

■Under most conditions, I would not go to closing with a tenant still in the house. If you have talked to the tenant and you are persuaded that they have already signed a lease for another place and are ready to move out, that is a reasonable assurance. But, unless you are absolutely sure that this is going to happen, I would leave the responsibility up to the seller to deliver an empty house.

Also, my comfort level would depend somewhat on how quickly I could get an eviction in the jurisdiction.

How do we dispel rumors being spread in the neighborhood about our family?

We have just moved into a new neighborhood. Somehow the word has gotten around that we are all dope users and drunks. I have no idea how all this got started. They won't let their children play with my children because of it. I suggested to my husband that we have an open house so that our neighbors can see differently. He disagrees and says it opens up the privacy of our home.

■Nonsense, I am on your side. Lets start with a premise - you are not the things they say. I would say, "Look, for whatever reason there has been some idle gossip about me and my family that is not true. We can understand how that might start, but we want to scotch it because we want to be good neighbors and we want you to drop over for a cup of coffee and get acquainted."

You will be meeting the problem head on. Tell your husband you're not going to open up your personal lives to everyone, but you do take exception to people talking behind your back and saying things that are not true. Why not invite the people who have accused you of these things? Tell your neighbors you would like them to confront you. If they really believe what they are saying, promise them in advance you won't sue. But, what you want is for them to come forward and say those things to your face. I would do it, you have nothing to lose.

❝ When they offer you a choice between a cash rebate and a reduced price, you are much better off taking the reduced price. **❞**

How can I get a TV repair shop to provide a loaner while they fix our warranteed set?

We bought my elderly parents a new TV. Well, it sparked and quit and the one the dealer replaced it with just quit too. Mother called them to check on the progress of the repairs and three people at the shop have admitted that she got a bad set. My mother is without a TV and afraid that the same trouble will happen again when they bring the set back. She's been without it for three weeks. Now they're waiting on a part. They said it is not their policy to provide a loaner TV, but I think it's only fair after all the trouble she's had.

■You say "Fine, I will rent a set and take the cost off the bill." Three weeks is too long for them to take without accommodating you, somehow.

I can understand why your mother may be afraid of these things and not trusting of their work. But, you can point out to her, in all likelihood, she has probably been involved in one or more automobiles accidents, but that did not stop her from riding in automobiles. Because the set gave her problems does not mean it will happen again. They have a right to try and repair it and send it to her home. After three weeks though, they should come up with a loaner for her. For $10 a week you can rent a TV. Go rent a TV tomorrow.

How can I get a refund on a small swing that is unsafe for our child?

When my daughter swings in it, the back legs come up off the ground. We explained this to the salesperson and he just said that she was too big for the swing and shouldn't be using it. We said if that was the case, we would like a refund. He said no way. There is no height/weight restriction in the literature. We purchased it on a credit card. Should I tell the credit card company that we don't want to pay for it?

■I think this purchase is a legitimate situation to put into contest. I do not usually subscribe to that point of view, but since the equipment was obviously not appropriate for your child and you relied on the salesperson's expertise in making the purchase, I would not hesitate to put it into contest. That means you take your swing right to the credit card company and tell them that the merchandise that was sold to you is inappropriate. Look at the back of your credit card bill and it will tell you how to put an item into contest. This can also be done by mail.

How can I get the builder of my custom home to replace a faulty roof?

I have a pitched roof and shingles keep blowing off. From what I can see, little papers on the back of the shingles should have been removed when the shingles were put down. In the three years that I have been in the house, I have had shingles come off three times. This time, I have had about one hundred square feet come off. The builder only gave me a one year warranty.

■That is a lot of roofing to blow off. I would think you have recourse. A roof generally has a minimum of a ten-year guarantee. If the shingles were put down properly, they should stay on. One of the problems is that cold weather is not a good time to put a roof on. You can have problems with the adhesive. But your problem should be correctable. I would start with the builder. Let them know that since they put the roof on they are responsible to make it right.

What is the purpose of a manufacturer's rebate?

Why not sell the item for $90.00 instead of $100.00 and get it over with? Why do they make me mail in their $10.00 coupon? And on a car you can get a huge rebate - why not just reduce the purchase price?

■If you made the price $90.00, that is all they would get for every one of those items. With a rebate, they're betting that a certain number of people won't send in the coupon. So they have, in effect, sold the item for the full price, while the retailer benefits from advertising the lower price.

The car is a little different matter. Frequently, they will give you the rebate if you do not take financing. When they offer you a choice between a cash rebate and a reduced price, you are much better off taking the reduced price. You have to pay tax on the money you receive. Furthermore, if you pay sales tax in your state, the lower price reduces the sales tax, so you save there as well.

What's the best way to let a company know that I am displeased with the workmanship evident in their product?

I had trouble with a pop-up camper I recently purchased. Apparently, one of the cables was too short, so a worker simply put a U-clamp on it. I am not going to ask for any money, I just want to express my gut feeling about this.

■I would write a letter to the CEO of the company. If it's a big company, go to the library and you will find them listed. Write a polite letter and let them know how you feel. It still comes down to the guy who puts the bolt on at the assembly line taking pride in what he does. Many people just don't have it.

Believe me though, the CEO of that company knows about the problem. He goes home at night and probably breaks out in a cold sweat thinking about it. Anybody who runs a business has got to have those fears. You should let him know that you are aware of the problem too. That fact will go a long way in promoting change.

What cautions would you have about buying by mail order?

I would like to buy an amateur radio transmitter. I have friends who have purchased from this company but I don't feel right sending $1,000 through the mail.

■Well, you're sitting there in an urban area, why in the world can't you walk into a place where you can see, feel, touch, smell and fondle, before you buy. I would feel far more comfortable making that size purchase from a store I could walk into, get a feel for the owner, check out their credentials and then, when or if something goes wrong, I'd have a place to go back to. It is very difficult to go back to the post office or mailbox and try to get your money back.

ADJUSTABLE RATE MORTGAGE (ARM)

A mortgage in which the interest is not fixed as in a traditional mortgage, but is adjusted to reflect the "cost of money". The mortgage is keyed to a specific indicator, such as a treasury bond index, and adjusted on an annual or biannual basis, or however a contract specifies. Ordinarily there is a "cap", or a limit, which the mortgage cannot exceed. However, a cap is not required. Without it, a mortgage can just moves with the market.

AMORTIZATION

The gradual repayment of a loan in periodic (usually monthly) payments, in which part of the money goes to principal and the remainder goes to loan interest on a decreasing basis. As the payments continue, more and more money goes toward principal and less toward interest, and if it is set up conventionally, the loan balance will be zero at the end of the term (an exception is a "balloon mortgage").

ANNUAL PERCENTAGE RATE (APR)

The total finance charge of a loan per year, expressed as a percentage. Oftentimes, you will see a rate indicated at 8%, and an APR at 8.3%. The extra money is a result of taking into account "points", application fees and so forth, all of which must be considered as interest when expressing the true interest rate.

APPRAISED VALUE

An estimate of property value made by a trained professional. This is not to be confused with an assessed value, which is set by a taxing authority. Usually, there is little or no relationship between "assessed value" and appraised value.

ASSESSED VALUE

The value set on property by taxing authorities in order to determine your real estate taxes. Frequently, the assessed value has no real relation to the true value or "market value" of the property. This is not a problem as long as the assessed value is determined to be correctly proportioned to the other properties in your community. It can be troublesome in that an assessed evaluation, at very best, is a subjective judgment and oftentimes, because of the magnitude of the job, errors do occur.

BALLOON MORTGAGE

One in which monthly payments are insufficient to repay the full amount of the loan within the set term. The result is a large lump sum balance due at the end of the term. For example; payments are set as if the mortgage were to be paid off in 25 or 30 years. However, at the end of a fixed period, say 5 years, the entire balance is payable. Most people cannot come up with this kind of money from their own resources. Customarily, a balloon is given by an owner to facilitate a sale and gives the buyer a longer period of time to seek out a long term mortgage. Also, from the buyer's perspective, more favorable terms may be available in the future than at the time the original balloon mortgage was written.

BANKS, COMMERCIAL BANKS, SAVINGS & LOANS, BUILDING & LOANS

All are institutions that have two basic functions: they encourage saving and make loans. Commercial banks are chartered by both the state and the federal government. Savings & loans and other similar institutions are more often chartered only by the state in which they function. It is of major import that depositors determine whether the institution they choose is insured by the federal government. Commercial banks are FDIC insured (Federal Depository Insurance Corporation), and the others are FSLIC insured (Federal Savings & Loan Insurance Corporation). Be certain the institution is federally insured, not just insured, as many states have private or state insurance companies which are not as solid as the federal insurance companies. There is no purpose here in detailing the distinctions between savings banks. Just remember that from the customer's point of view, the primary thing to determine is whether or not it is a federally insured institution. If it is, your deposits are always safe up to $100,000.

BROKER - A person who acts as the intermediary between a buyer and a seller. There are many types of brokers, including real estate, insurance, stock, business, and others. Their function is to bring a willing buyer and a willing seller together. In the case of real estate, the seller usually pays the broker's fee. When you are buying a product through an insurance broker or a stock broker, you will pay a commission. It is either included in the price or added on. It is important to recognize that the broker's loyalty is to the person or firm paying his commission.

CAP - Term used in adjustable rate mortgages. It limits the percentage of change in interest rate over the life of the contract. Customarily, it also limits the increases or decreases during each adjustment period.

CLOSED END LEASE - A lease which allows the lessee to either walk away with no further obligation or purchase the property at a specific, pre-agreed-upon, price. This price is usually derived from an index formula or publication. This type of contract frequently applies to the leasing of automobiles. It should be noted that when leasing an automobile, more often than not, there is a limitation to the annual mileage. If this limitation is exceeded, the lessee must pay an additional fee.

CLOSING COSTS - Costs due at closing or settlement, which usually include "origination fee" or "points", the cost of your attorney, the cost of "title insurance", taxes that are due, and adjustments owed to the previous owner (for things like oil left in his tank, taxes that have been pre-paid, or a pre-payment of a hazard policy on the home, which is ordinarily one quarter of the taxes in advance). Be certain to go over this with your attorney well in advance, so that you are prepared to pay the amount necessary at closing, otherwise, the deal cannot be consummated.

COLLISION DAMAGE WAIVER - Insurance, without regard to fault,

against liability in the event that rented vehicles - both cars and trucks - are damaged. You will find that collision damage waivers are very expensive, so check with your insurance broker. It is likely that if you carry insurance on your car, it will cover a rental vehicle as well, making a collision damage waiver redundant. By declining this insurance you can save significantly on your rental fees. Be certain to be guided by the expert knowledge of your insurance agent or broker.

CONDOMINIUM (commonly known as "condo") - An individually owned unit in a multiple unit building on which you pay the taxes. All central areas (elevators, roofs, parking lots, etc.) are owned collectively by the condominium owners. Through the condominium association, you will be responsible for taxes on commonly owned property, the maintenance of that property and attendant expenses. Be certain to note that when purchasing or renting a condominium, you may have to pay additional fees to use recreational areas such as pools, tennis courts, and so forth. This is not always the case, but it is absolutely essential that you inquire. It is also important to note that a condominium owner usually can sell without the permission of the other condo owners.

CONTRACT FOR DEED - An arrangement whereby the title remains in the seller's name. Usually this is done because the buyer cannot arrange for independent financing. The new owner pays either the seller or the mortgage holder directly. There is a danger in paying the mortgage holder directly because it puts the lender on notice that a third party has become involved in the transaction. Frequently, this violates the "due on sale" clause. This means that if a property changes ownership, the entire mortgage becomes payable at that time. Be certain, if you are entering into an arrangement of this kind, that your attorney has carefully scrutinized the contract and assures you that it does not violate a loan agreement.

164 CO-OPERATIVE (commonly known as "co-op") - A building owned by a corporation, usually owned by the residents of that building. Each resident owns shares of stock in the corporation. The number of shares that a resident owns reflects the desirability of the apartment and his percentage ownership of the building. For example, if the building has two apartments, one a one-bedroom, the other a two-bedroom, the second owner might own two shares of stock while the first owner might own one: a total of three shares. There are many other variables that enter into valuation. For example, location of the apartment in the building (higher level apartments sell for more than lower level apartments in major cities), the number of rooms, the view, the location of the building and so forth. It is important to note that in most cooperative arrangements, the other owners must approve the sale of shares to a buyer. This can be troublesome, in many instances, where the board of directors is very fussy about who purchases the apartments, although it could be argued that this helps maintain the value and integrity of the unit.

CO-SIGNER - A person who signs a loan note in addition to the borrower because the lender feels the person borrowing the money is not creditworthy. If you are asked to co-make or guarantee a loan, be absolutely certain that you understand that you are as responsible as the maker of the loan. This means that you could be held accountable for the entire amount of monies borrowed if the borrower defaults, even though you didn't receive a penny. Further understand that the lender will likely go after that person from whom it deems easiest to collect. More often than not, this is not the original borrower, but the co-signer. This is not meant to discourage you, but to make you aware of the fact that you are very vulnerable when co-signing a loan for anyone.

EQUITY - The value of a financial interest, after the mortgage has been subtracted from the market value of the property. If the property has a fair market value of $100,000, and you have a $75,000 mortgage, your equity then is $25,000.

ESCROW - Funds set aside for a specific purpose. When the terms of that purpose are met, the money can be drawn out. When one is purchasing a home, frequently the lender will require an escrow account to be certain that there are funds sufficient to pay the taxes, insurance, and other assessments against the property. Customarily, these are recurring charges. A portion of your monthly mortgage payments would go into this account, and usually, no interest is paid on it. When purchasing a home, if there is a deficiency of some nature (perhaps the sidewalk has a crack in it), it is customary to have the seller put a certain amount of money in escrow until the repairs are paid. In the event that the repairs are not made, this money is given to the buyer.

FEDERAL HOUSING ADMINISTRATION (FHA) - A federal agency under the Department of Housing and Urban Development which insures mortgages for lenders, ordinarily on residential housing. They will guarantee $67,500 to $90,000, depending on the jurisdiction. You can learn more about your jurisdiction from your local FHA office or by calling the central number in Washington, D.C. at (202) 426-7212. Many sellers are not agreeable to FHA financing because of the additional paperwork and the restrictions.

FEE APPRAISER - An individual who, for a fixed fee, makes a professional judgment as to what a particular piece of property is worth. These individuals are usually a member of, but not limited to, associations such as The Society of Real Estate Appraisers or the American Institute of Real Estate Appraisers. The most common method of appraisal is a "comparables" method, where the fee appraiser examines similar properties in the area, notes recent sale prices and uses these numbers to determine the value of the property being appraised. Appraisal is never to be confused with assessment.

FEE SIMPLE - The sole ownership of a clear title of real estate. It is also known as sole tenancy. Most people purchase real estate in fee simple. Other arrangements include leases. The property under the building is never sold, but leased for a specified period, say 99 years. Also, in some portions of our country, people enter into what is called a "contract for deed".

FIXED-RATE MORTGAGE - A "traditional" mortgage with a fixed interest rate. The rate is established, and for the term of the mortgage, say 25 or 30 years, it does not change. Because the monthly payment remains the same, many people are more comfortable with this than the Adjustable Rate Mortgage (ARM). It is also possible to refinance it at a better rate, if mortgage rates drop substantially. It should be noted, however, that refinancing can be an expensive venture and in many states it is proper for the lender to put in a pre-payment penalty for as many as five years after the original loan is made. Be certain that you understand all of the terms prior to signing a mortgage.

GARNISHMENT - A court order that requires an employer to pay a portion of the wages of the debtor-employee directly to a creditor to satisfy a debt. The specified sum will be deducted each pay period until the debtor's account is settled. Not all states permit garnishment. You should find out if you live in a garnishee state, and if an obligation can be settled by garnishment, whether you are a debtor or a creditor. Unfortunately, many employers will fire an employee rather than go through the hassle of garnishment. As a debtor, it is certainly to be avoided if at all possible.

HEALTH MAINTENANCE ORGANIZATION (HMO) - A medical organization which offers its members a wide variety of health services in exchange for a predetermined fee, usual-

ly paid on a monthly or quarterly basis. This differs from conventional insurance in many ways, but the primary difference is that HMOs have their own medical staff and facilities. Like everything else, Hmos have both advantages and disadvantages. One of the huge disadvantages is that you are frequently limited to the hospitals and medical people that the HMO selects, unless very specialized services are necessary. On the plus side, Hmos are geared toward health maintenance and preventative medicine. Since the cost remains the same regardless of the number of visits or medical procedures, there is a higher motivation for check-up visits which might not ordinarily be made. While this can be a health advantage, it can also be the reason for extensive waits, both for an appointment date and while in the doctor's office. The major disadvantage, as I see it, is that most HMOs are of a clinical nature and can lack the personal touch that the private physician can offer. Even though the HMO is, in my opinion, usually impersonal, many folks are highly pleased with the way they operate.

HOME OWNER'S INSURANCE - A package policy that has basic coverage, insuring the structure of a house against fire, lightning, freezing water pipes, and so forth. Also there is protection for the home owner against loss of personal property from burglary, fire, etc., and injury or damages to others for which the home owner would be liable. Be certain to discuss this carefully with your insurance agent, or broker, since in most jurisdictions there are several forms of home owner's policies, some more comprehensive than others. Obviously, the more comprehensive, the more costly.

INDEX - The measurement by which an adjustable mortgage rate is changed. If the index rises, the interest rate will rise, and if the index falls, the rate will fall. The index is often based on the price of U.S. Treasury instruments, which accurately reflects the "cost of money", as opposed to an artificial index such as the CPI (Consumer Price Index), which is set by various individuals and agencies.

INTESTATE OR INTESTACY - The death of an individual without a valid "will". Without a will, the assets acquired during a lifetime are distributed according to the laws of that state, province or jurisdiction. It should be noted that in many states, the children receive the bulk of the estate, even though it might be your desire that your spouse receive the entire proceeds of your estate. This and other major decisions may be made in direct contrast to the choices the deceased would have made. It is never wise to be without a will. In my opinion, it is equally essential to have an attorney draw the document according to the laws of the state where the majority of your assets are held.

LEASE - A contract between an owner and a tenant or renter of real property which spells out the obligations of each. It is usually for a longer period of time than a "month-to-month rental" and is always in writing. The typical landlord lease is skewed with advantages for the landlord rather than the tenant. While it can be somewhat arduous, it is advisable for you to read over the lease before entering into it. Pay particular attention to your rights for subletting (in the event that you wish to leave early), and to penalties with regard to wear and tear of property and to other tenant responsibilities.

LIEN - A legal claim of a lender against a borrower's property, which has been pledged as security for a debt. If a debt is not paid as agreed, the lien holder can sometimes force the sale of the property to pay the debt. Most liens are in the form of mortgages. However, if you own property, and judgment is found against you, the person holding the judgment can file a lien against any real property in your name. In that case, the property cannot be sold and equity distributed to the owner, without this lien being satisfied.

LIMITED PARTNERSHIP - An agreement between one or more general partners, and one or more other partners whose liability is limited to the amount of money which they have invested in a company. The general partners are the guys who put the deal together and are responsible for the monies and operation of the partnership. The limited partner has no voice in management, but his liability is a fixed amount, unlike the general partner, who enjoys no such limitation. Limited partnerships allow the small investor to be involved in bigger investment vehicles. For example, suppose you want to buy a building and you need $100,000 in capital. If there are twenty limited partners, then each only needs to put $5,000 into the pot. The general partners may put in little or no money, but they provide the expertise. The lynch-pin of any limited partnership is the general partner. His ability and integrity are the key ingredients to look for and be aware of.

LOAD - The securities industry word for commission. It is the amount paid to a salesman for selling you a product. Low-load is a discount commission, and no-load is an investment vehicle where no commission is paid. This also means that there is no salesman, and you must go to the company and arrange the sale yourself.

MAINTENANCE CHARGE - Common charges, which can be attributed to a building's expenses, such as real estate taxes and the care and upkeep of that building. When you buy a condominium or enter into a cooperative, be sure to understand that there will be these extra charges above and beyond your mortgage costs. If you own your home, you pay maintenance charges out of your pocket, but as a member of the condominium or cooperative association, the maintenance charge is assessed.

MARKET VALUE - A price which is mutually agreed upon. It's the lowest price a seller is willing to accept, and at the same time, the highest price a buyer is willing to pay.

MONEY MARKET MUTUAL FUNDS

The term "money market" has been used by banks and other lenders to describe a specific type of investment vehicle, whereby the management invests in ordinarily short-term vehicles such as, but not limited to, Euro-dollars, jumbo bank CDs, commercial paper, and short-term marketable assets. Your share value customarily remains in one dollar units and deposits are expressed in shares, so that if you deposit $1,000, you then own 1000 shares. You do not have $1,000 on deposit.

MONTH-TO-MONTH RENTAL

The monthly compensation for the use of property, which can ordinarily be terminated by either party with thirty days notice (as opposed to a "lease").

MORTGAGE

A document, held by a lender, which proves legal claim to property; a security for money borrowed.

MORTGAGE INSURANCE

A form of life insurance. The name "mortgage insurance" has been used to encourage people with a mortgage debt to buy life insurance. Generally, but not always, it is decreasing term insurance. This means that as the mortgage is paid down, the amount of insurance grows smaller in step with the "amortization" of your mortgage. It is wise to shop for mortgage insurance as policies do vary.

MUTUAL FUND

A combining of many investors assets into one professionally managed investment pool. Customarily, the managers take a percentage of the fund's gross receipts each year as their expenses and profits, as opposed to a percentage of the profits. In other words, whether the fund earns or loses, the management will exact a percentage fee for the administration of the fund.

NET WORTH

The total assets minus the total liabilities. Put together everything you have... your house, your business, money in the bank, securities and whatever, add them all up and subtract your debts. If you come up with a negative number, you're in deep trouble.

NOW ACCOUNT

It stands for Negotiable Order of Withdrawal. As far as the consumer is concerned, it smells like a checking account, looks like a checking account and acts like a checking account. In some jurisdictions, institutions other than commercial banks were not allowed to issue checks, so negotiable order of withdrawal accounts were created. NOW accounts and indeed some checking accounts will pay interest on balances over a certain amount. Understand that all checking and NOW accounts are not created equal. It is wise to shop. One institution may have a very good deal for someone who writes only a few checks, another for one who writes a lot, a third for senior citizens and a fourth for students. Banking is now a very competitive enterprise and all products should be looked at carefully.

ORIGINATION FEE

The fee that a lender charges the borrower to cover some of the costs of issuing a loan. In addition to this fee, the borrower is frequently charged a fee for credit application, inspection appraisals, and other attendant costs to the lender. While the origination fee is paid at closing and only when the mortgage is granted, many of the other fees are paid up-front, and are not refunded even if the mortgage is denied.

PRIVATE MORTGAGE INSURANCE (PMI)

Insurance which allows the purchaser to buy a home or other property with less than the required down-payment, which is usually 20%. In the event that you default, the insurance company will protect the loss to the lender from 0% to 20%. This is a fancy way of saying you are paying an insurance company to become your "co-signer" for the first 20% of the loan. This can be paid in one lump sum or with a down-payment and monthly installments. You must be certain to determine which is better for you. If you know that you will hold the property for a long period of time, sometimes the bulk payment is desirable. More often than not, it is to your advantage to pay the down-payment and the monthly installments, bearing in mind that once your equity increases to over 20% (by virtue of appreciation or additions to the property), you may apply to the lender to have the PMI requirement dropped, at which time your payments to the private mortgage insurance company would cease.

POINTS (also known as "discount points") - A one-time additional charge paid at a closing which theoretically covers the cost of processing a mortgage. Each point is 1% of the mortgage. It is a way to encourage the lender to loan you the money. Points are considered pre-paid interest and increase the initial costs in order to decrease finance charges. The cost of the points is included in the APR. On FHA and VA mortgages, the amount of points the buyer may pay is limited by law, but there is no limit to how much the seller can be charged.

QUIT CLAIM - The release by one individual of all rights and titles to a piece of real property. Understand, this does not release you, the individual, from any responsibility that you may have by being party to a mortgage. Even though you give up your rights, you cannot relinquish your responsibility. If the other party stops paying a mortgage, you must continue, because you may be held responsible for the deficiency. As I see it, you have a couple of alternatives. You can sell your portion of the property to your partner and have him refinance the property (releasing you of any responsibility), or request the lender to remove your name from the bond. Remember, the lender has no obligation to honor your request.

RIGHT OF FIRST REFUSAL - A mechanism which allows a party to have the first chance to say no. It is often given to tenants renting a piece of real estate. For example, if you are going to sell the property and you are offered $100 for it, you, as the landlord, must first go to the tenants and ask them if they would like to pay $100 for the property. They have a short period of time, say ten days, to exercise this right of first refusal. This is not to be confused with an "option to purchase".

RIGHT OF SURVIVORSHIP -The right of a surviving co-owner of a piece of property to legally inherit the interest of a deceased co-owner. Oftentimes, it is expedient to put ownership in more than one name. For example, an elderly parent is unable to attend to his or her own affairs due to disability, so another name is added to the bank account. The intent is to give you access to the account in order to use the funds in your parent's best interest. However, legally you are a co-owner of the money. If it is written with the right of survivorship, all the money belongs to you in the event that your parent dies. Understand that this does not reduce your tax liability, but it does facilitate access to the money. Right of survivorship should not be confused with "tenants in common". If you are in doubt, take the time to discuss it with the appropriate bank official and/or your attorney.

TENANCY BY ENTIRETY - Ownership restricted to husband and wife, generally used for real estate, and held in both names. In the instance of either one's death, the entire property belongs to the other. Neither can sell their interest without the consent of the other. Tenancy by entirety is only available in a limited number of states. Check your own state laws regarding availability.

TITLE INSURANCE - Insurance which always covers against defects in title, so that any question of ownership is settled by the title company at their expense. Sometimes, title insurance coverage diminishes with the "amortization" of the loan. This is not desirable. In some jurisdictions, as is the case in Florida, it is required that the seller pay for title insurance. However, it is customary for the buyer to pay for it in most places. Your attorney will usually arrange for title insurance.

UNDIVIDED INTEREST - Property jointly owned by two or more people. For example, suppose that a piece of property is left to three or four children in a will. All four children own the house together, but no one can say "I own the bedroom," etc. The problem with this arrangement is that if one or more of the owners wants to sell but another owner does not, it oftentimes takes a court and a lot of money to straighten it out. Ordinarily, it is not a good idea to leave property undivided. It is far better to appoint a personal representative or executor in your will to dispose of the property and divide the money. Another approach might be to order the executor to dispose of the property, giving the heirs "right of first refusal".

VETERANS ADMINISTRATION (VA) - An agency of the federal government designed to help veterans. One such service helps veterans get long term, low down-payment mortgages. The lender must follow VA guidelines in order to have a portion of the loan guaranteed against loss. Many sellers are reluctant to enter into VA arrangements because of the additional red-tape and time involved in having the loan approved. Furthermore, they are often obliged to pay a greater portion of the "points" because the law limits the amount a veteran may pay.

WILL (also known as a last will and testament) - A legal document which directs how acquired assets will be distributed among whomever is named to share in the estate. A will should always be drawn up by an attorney. In the event that one does·not have a will, one is deemed to have died "intestate".

BUSINESS

CAREERS-EMPLOYMENT

INVESTMENTS

LANDLORD-TENANT-NEIGHBOR

LEGAL

TAX QUESTIONS